RATTLESNAKES & ROUTE 66

Thanks, Mary :)

JOHN CLARK

Printed in the United States of America

This edition Printed, 2020

© John Clark, 2020

Cover Art © *The Dust Jacket Designs*, 2020
Editing © *John Clark*, 2020
Interior Design © *Foundation Formatting/The Dust Jacket Designs*, 2020

All rights reserved.

Without limiting the rights under copyright reserved above, no part of this publication may be reproduced, stored in or introduced into a retrieval system, or transmitted, in any form or by any means (electronic, mechanical, photocopying, recording, or otherwise) without the prior written permission of the copyright owner.

The scanning, uploading, and distribution of this book via the Internet or via any other means without the permission of the copyright owner is illegal and punishable by law. Please purchase only authorized electronic editions and do not participate in or encourage piracy of copyrighted materials. Your support of the author's rights is appreciated.

Table of Contents

Introduction II
Chapter One 1
Chapter Two 5
Chapter Three 10
Chapter Four 15
Chapter Five 20
Chapter Six 25
Chapter Seven 29
Chapter Eight 33
Chapter Nine 37
Chapter Ten 41
Chapter Eleven 46
Chapter Twelve 50
Chapter Thirteen 54
Chapter Fourteen 59
Chapter Fifteen 64
Chapter Sixteen 69
Chapter Seventeen 73
Chapter Eighteen 78
Chapter Nineteen 83
Conclusion 87
A Small Favor to Ask 89
About the Author 91
More from John H. Clark III 93

Introduction

When someone sits across the table from you, looks you straight in the eye, and says with complete sincerity that not only do they believe in angels, but they have seen supernatural spirits up close and personal more than once during their life, you have a choice to make – either believe what they are saying, or quietly smile and nod while maybe questioning their sanity.

In the case of Drew Meeks and her sister, Andrea, two grown, successful, and intelligent women from small-town central Texas, not only do both say they have seen and been visited by angels, but that other-worldly visitors are all around, all the time, and anyone has the ability to see them.

"You don't have to believe it at all," Andrea says. "It is what it is. That's the thing. I don't think I'm different from anybody else, really. I think I pay attention more.

"I never try to convince anybody of anything, but if you start researching, you'll start to see that these things are happening to everybody. You'll start to understand. If you pay attention to the little things that happen in your life, the things that you call coincidences, you can figure it out. It's not really hard."

Interviewing Drew and Andrea is but one of the highlights of my 30-year journalism career. I have written all kinds of stories about all kinds of people, places and things – happy stories, sad stories, tragic stories, inspiring stories. The thing is, no matter who you are, where you come from, how mundane and boring anyone's life may seem, everyone has an interesting story, whether they realize it or not.

One sunny afternoon, I was visiting with a guy named Mike Reed for a newspaper feature story about his massive comic book collection. When I went to his house, the Alabama native and U.S. Army veteran was proudly showing me samples from a large bookcase in a spare bedroom that included thousands and thousands of reprints of vintage comics dating back as far as 1936.

As he was talking, Mike casually mentioned something about his childhood:

"We never lived in the same place longer than six months, if we stayed that long," the 59-year-old said. "I've got (seven) brothers and sisters that were born from Virginia to New Mexico. When my stepfather was around, he was drunk, knocked all of us around.

"I saw him beat my mother to death when I was 10 years old. I just finally decided ... you've got to leave all that stuff behind you and go on. I can't change any of it."

Without skipping a beat, Mike went on talking about his comics, but I stopped him in his tracks.

"Hang on," I said, holding up my hand. "Can we go back for a second?"

Never knowing his biological father, his mother now dead, and stepfather in prison, the young boy was sent to live at a children's home, where he stayed from fourth grade through high school, until he joined the military when he was 19 and went on to a successful life.

An interview that started out to be about comic books turned into a gut-wrenching story of triumph over tragedy.

That kind of thing happens a lot when I'm interviewing people. Some off-hand comment takes things in a completely different direction. Sometimes, the interview is not going well and it looks like the story might turn out to be a dud, when voila! The magic happens.

You just gotta listen.

Thanks for taking a look at this book.

All these stories started out as newspaper columns when I wrote for a paper called the Copperas Cove Banner, where I won a first-place award from the South Texas Press Association, a terrific honor.

I think you're going to like it.

Enjoy.

Chapter One

Reflections of war

Tears well up in Nelson "Smitty" Schmidt's 91-year-old eyes as he thinks back to his service during World War II – the things he saw and was required to do.

"Life is terribly cheap in war," the father of five, grandfather of 15 and great-grandfather of six said. "For someone who has been brought up to believe in the sanctity of human life, it's a huge change.

"We would laugh at things that weren't funny, but it was either do that or go nuts. Nobody goes into combat and comes out the same way."

Schmidt, better known throughout central Texas by his nickname, Smitty, was a participant two months ago in the Honor Flight program, a non-profit group that works to transport military veterans from across the country to Washington, D.C., to be recognized and to visit the various war memorials there, in and around the National Mall.

The longtime owner and operator of Smitty's Texaco on the corner of Avenue D and Main Street in downtown Copperas Cove, Schmidt said he has been to Washington, D.C., a number of times before and seen the memorials, so he wasn't sure at first if he wanted to make the trip, but an old familiar sense of duty – along with encouragement from his daughter, Sylvia, who signed him up – finally tipped the scales.

"I have never participated in a parade; never joined a veteran's organization," Smitty said. "I made up in my head early in the game that I was doing a job, (and) I happened to be the right age at the right time, and I'm glad I was able to do it, but I never considered myself to be any kind of hero. Didn't want to be a hero.

"I thought about it up and down for a day or two, and one

thing they said was that they were trying to get as many World War II vets as they could, because we're pretty much an endangered species. There's not a whole lot of us left.

"So, I decided to go ahead and go."

When his flight from Austin arrived in Washington, Smitty and a group of fellow veterans traveling with him were treated like the heroes that they truly are, with a color guard and bagpipes player leading them through the airport, and hundreds of people on hand to welcome them, along with police escorts through the city.

"All of us World War II vets were in wheelchairs, and the oldest person in our group, she was 96 or 97 – she apparently was an Army nurse – and she was walking behind her wheelchair, pushing it," he said, smiling. "She said she didn't have to ride in that thing; she didn't need anybody pushing her around. Finally, the lady that was with her convinced her she needed to get in the wheelchair.

"There must have been a thousand people there running up and shaking your hand, thanking you. They hauled us around in buses with police escorts, and we went through town faster than I've ever gone through D.C.," he said, laughing. "Almost made you feel like you were somebody."

While Smitty and I sat in his living room talking about the trip, his wife of 45 years, Charlene, kept bringing out scrapbooks and other mementos, including a collection of photographs from a reunion several years ago for the 548th Anti-Aircraft Automatic Weapons Battalion, his unit from the war.

As he pointed out old Army buddies, memories and stories came flooding back.

"That's the guy I pitched my pup tent with in France, when we first landed there. He had curly red hair at the time. For some reason, he's turned kind of gray now," Smitty said, smiling. "All those guys have changed – they've gotten old! They haven't stayed young, like me. I don't understand it.

"This old boy here had kind of an interesting story. The Germans were known for being very methodical in everything they did. And on the banks of the Ruhr river, it was full of anti-tank mines and anti-personnel mines.

"They had their way of laying them out, and a day or two after we got across the river, our engineers were digging up mines that were on the side the Germans had been occupying. Once you figured out the pattern of how they laid those mines, you knew exactly where to look for the next one.

"So, they got to this guy and his foxhole, and they said, 'Hey, fella, what did you do with the mine?' He said, 'What mine?' They said, 'The one that was right where you dug your foxhole.' He said, 'There wasn't no mine here.'

"They said, 'There had to be.' But for some reason, they had failed to put one in that spot."

Schmidt was born in 1925 in the Meier Settlement community, about 10 miles from Riesel, near Waco, and moved around the state as his father, E.E. Schmidt, pastored various Methodist churches. He started and finished school in Copperas Cove – Miss Jewell Yarborough (Oct. 21, 1890 – Dec. 2, 1994) was his first teacher – graduating with a class of 15 students, five boys and 10 girls, in 1943.

Shortly after graduation, he turned 18 and was drafted by the military. He and a buddy who was also called to service wanted to become paratroopers, but Schmidt wound up assigned to anti-aircraft artillery training and learned to fire 40 mm and Quad-50 machine guns.

When his unit eventually sailed for Europe in 1944, his ship anchored off the coast of Omaha Beach for several weeks awaiting their orders to unload. It was a sobering sight, looking at the aftermath of the famed D-Day invasion that had taken place earlier. An estimated 2,400 Americans died when troops stormed the beach.

The memory still brings a tear to his eye and a lump to his throat.

"I'd see those machine gun placements high up in those bluffs, and I cried sometimes, thinking about those poor devils with nothing to hide behind. I had a friend who was in the medics when they landed on D-Day, and that old boy told me, 'We had so many dead bodies there (that) we just stacked 'em up, and that gave us a little protection.'"

Although he has always been reluctant to accept accolades for his military service, and has his share of painful memories, Smitty is nevertheless proud of some things he was able to accomplish back then.

"It's hard to explain," he said, pausing at times to compose himself and wipe away tears.

"I was one of the few (in his unit) who spoke German fluently, so I was able to conduct business with the people there, as we came in contact with them. At first, I hated it with a passion – I really did.

"Our orders were, when you get to where you're gonna spend the night, if you find a house that's good enough to live in, you move the people out of it and you take it over. Most of the civilians we came in contact with were middle-aged to elderly people, and a big percentage of them had no idea what was going on.

"All my ancestors came from Europe, so except for the guts that my ancestors had to leave everything they knew and come to America, that could have been me and my parents out there. So I hated doing that. I thought, 'Why in the heck did I have to learn German?' I did not like doing what I was having to do.

"But I got to thinking about it, and I thought, 'Well, at least I can explain to the people what to expect.' Like if we had to take over a house … have you ever been in a nursing home and seen how the eyes of a lot of those old people are empty?

"These people … you'd go down the highway and you'd see some of them going this way and some of them going that way. Most of them had grabbed a few little things and they'd put them in a little wagon or on a bike, and they're walking along with that same blank expression. That same look in their eyes. And that hurt, for me.

"I got to thinking, and I preached to my buddies, I said, 'When we get in contact with civilians, treat those people with courtesy. Try to treat people like you would want your parents to be treated.'

"Our gun crew, I'd say most of 'em were morally above average, and I got to where I decided I was going to try to leave any place I was going to have dealings with the civilian population, I wanted to leave a little island of good will. And I think I succeeded."

John Clark

A hero?
I think so.

Chapter Two

Always a Tiger

"Blood makes the grass grow."
"Pain is weakness leaving the body."
"Suck it up!"

Just a few familiar expressions that will forever remind Charlie Griggs of his glory days as a standout center and defensive end for Belton High School's championship football teams back in the late 1960s.

"Those were common sayings around the fieldhouse for as long as I can remember," said Griggs, a 1970 Belton graduate who earned first-team all-state honors his senior year.

"Players said them to other players, and coaches said them, too. Heard those sayings from most of my coaches."

Now 63 years old, Griggs was born in downtown Belton, Texas, roughly halfway between Austin and Waco along Interstate 35, at a hospital that is now a parking lot behind the old post office on Main Street, across from the Bell County Museum. His dad for a long time operated Griggs Equipment, a church and school furniture manufacturer that was once the largest employer in town.

Following his senior season, when the Tigers went undefeated in district play and advanced to the state semi-finals before losing a 10-6 heartbreaker to West Columbia at Kyle Field in College Station, Griggs received a slew of athletic scholarship offers from such places as the University of Texas, Arkansas, Notre Dame, Southern Methodist University, and Baylor.

He turned them all down.

"I really was just kind of tired of football," Griggs explained, sipping an iced tea on the patio of a coffee shop along the busy interstate that stretches more than 1,500 miles from Duluth, Minnesota down to Laredo, Texas, on the U.S.-Mexico border.

"All the old Southwest Conference schools were interested – a bunch of them, I couldn't have gotten into because my grades weren't good. SMU and Baylor, I couldn't have gotten into at the time. I think UT was taking anybody who had a pulse ... but I decided I didn't want to play.

"As time (for football season) got closer, I went down to Texas A&I in Kingsville and was going to play for them. But after a few workouts, I was, like, nah, this ain't for me."

He came back home, went to junior college in Temple for a while, but didn't much enjoy that, so he started working construction and ranching, got married to his high school sweetheart, and life went on.

Until one miserably hot summer day when Griggs decided maybe his chosen career path wasn't all it was cracked up to be.

"One day, I was welding on a place down here – this would have been 1976 or '77 – and it was 105 degrees; I was having to wear a leather cape, a leather hood and all that. I decided, 'I don't really like this so much.'

"I went home and told my wife that I thought I'd go back to school."

Griggs enrolled at the University of Mary Hardin-Baylor in Belton and graduated with honors in three years, then started a career in public school teaching that saw him spend three decades with the Belton school district before retiring five years ago. His wife, Julie, is also a retired school teacher.

His decision to put away the welding rod and enter the world of academia was apparently a pretty good one. Since he retired from teaching history, Griggs constantly runs into former students at restaurants, stores, ball games, just about anywhere and everywhere, who invariably greet their old teacher with a smile and a hug. Sure enough, as he and I were chatting last Saturday afternoon, a young lady walked by and Griggs called her name and they hugged and talked for several minutes, then posed together for a cellphone selfie.

"It's funny ... I've run into students in the strangest places. One time down on the Frio (River, at Garner State Park), I was just getting in the river, and this guy all the way across the river yelled, 'Mr. Griggs!' He's hollerin' and wadin' across the river, and we hugged. He's a pilot with Southwest Airlines now.

"I feel like my biggest accomplishment during my teaching career was letting kids know I cared about them. A bunch of these kids couldn't tell you a thing I taught 'em, but they'd tell you that I made them feel good.

"My first year, I tried to be a bad-ass, a hard-ass. I figured out about mid-term that I wasn't going to be able to do that. It just wasn't my nature, and I wasn't enjoying it. I've always been a person who enjoys laughing – got in trouble for it a lot in high school. So I started cracking jokes; doing things that were fun.

"There were always teachers that I thought taught better than me, but there wasn't anybody – I felt – that took care of my kids better than me.

"I've had kids tell me that they wouldn't have turned out the way they did if I hadn't talked to them in high school. Then, of course, there were the ones that I couldn't get through to; that I couldn't reach.

"I've had some who are doing life in prison for murder. I've had several of those. Those are the ones that I regret the most."

Listening to Mr. Griggs reminisce about his beloved hometown is surely what one of his history lessons must have been like for his students. His recollection of names and dates and places, and especially football games and football seasons, is encyclopedic.

"My senior year," he says, "we started out with Mexia, who we had lost to the year before. We beat them. Then we played Killeen at Killeen, and they were still loaded from the year before. They had guys who were going to play in the NFL.

"Our team had gone from a multi-threat, pass and run offense, to primarily a running team, and it did not work out well that year against Killeen. We lost 27-0, which was a big shock to our system, but at least it wasn't on Tiger Field.

"After that game, we ran off eight straight victories. Undefeated in district play again. The last game in district is against Lampasas, and whoever wins that game is going to be district champ.

"We go over there and beat them 36-0, and it wasn't even really that close. We didn't punt the whole game. We ran it down their throats – probably had 400 yards rushing. We had two real good running backs – three good running backs – one of them, Jim Stewart, is my brother-in-law now.

"I was about six-foot, 215 pounds, and we had one other lineman who weighed 200 pounds. Back then, kids weren't as big as they are now. A 200-pound lineman was a big lineman. I was big for my time period. We were bigger than most teams, but not as big as some.

"Anyway, after we beat Lampasas, we went and played Gregory Portland down at Bobcat Stadium in San Marcos again. They had a good team. Marty Akins was their quarterback, and he went on to play at UT (University of Texas).

"We were down 10-3, with about a minute and a half to play, and we were on the 30-yard line. We were cramming it down their throats, and scored with about 20 seconds to go, and we were ahead on penetrations (inside the 20-yard line), so we won the game.

"The next week, we played Kerrville-Tivy at San Marcos again. It was a deluge – the water was ankle-deep in one of the end zones. The fields weren't built to drain (water) like they are now. In that one end zone, if you were to go face-plant down there, you might drown before you got out. We beat them, 26-14.

"Then we went to Kyle Field in College Station and played West Columbia in the state semi-finals. They had a guy by the name of Charlie Davis, who went on to play for the University of Colorado and then the Cincinnati Bengals.

"We were behind 10-6, and we had the ball with less than a minute to go, on I think the 20-yard line. It was fourth-down and two yards to go for a first down, and we gave it to (David) Bartek up the middle, and they stopped him short. That was hard."

Although he lives now just up the highway in Temple, Griggs, father of two and grandfather of seven, will always call Belton home.

"I love the town. I have a brother who lives in Austin, and I have lots of friends who moved away, but I stayed around through the '80s to help with my dad, who was sick, and by the time I was 30, we had roots here, so we just stuck around.

"We just never saw any reason to leave."

Chapter Three

Beating the odds

When she got the bad news, Cindy Wilson's life was understandably shattered.

"I called the doctor, because I hadn't heard anything after two weeks. I said, 'Look, my results should be in by now.' The nurse took my name and said she would call me back.

"She calls back and says, 'Would you like to come in and talk to the doctor?'

"I said, 'No, you might as well just go ahead and tell me now.'

"She said, 'Yes, you do have cancer.' She said, 'I'm going to let you take it in for a few minutes, and I'll call you back.'

"I hung up the phone, and that's when it hit me. I just started bawling."

Cindy, a Killeen, Texas, native who was born at Darnall Army Community Hospital on nearby Fort Hood, was on the job at First National Bank Texas, where she works as an administrative assistant, when she took that life-changing phone call. The 45-year-old mother of one had suspected for about a month that something was seriously wrong.

"It was around February 2009," Cindy recalls. "I was 37 years old, and I just knew something was different on my right side, my right breast.

"I went to my doctor, and she says, 'No, you're fine.'

"About a week and a half later, I go back and I said, 'No, I'm not fine.' I didn't feel anything – there was no lump – but it was warm to the touch, and I just knew something was not right. I had done some research, and I said, 'I think I have inflammatory breast cancer.'

"She goes, 'No, with cancers, you don't get a warm feeling. Let's prescribe you some antibiotics, and we'll go from there.'

"I just started bawling. I said, 'No, something is not right.' Finally, she agreed, and she sent me to get a mammogram that same day. Then, I was set up for a biopsy, sonogram, and then two weeks later, I got the phone call saying I had cancer."

As co-workers tried their best to comfort her, one called Cindy's husband, Colen, at work and told him to hurry over to the bank.

"They said, 'You need to come get Cindy. She got a call from the doctor, and she's got cancer,'" Colen recalls. "I don't really remember what I thought, except that I needed to get there. I only worked two blocks from her, so I could get there pretty fast. Everybody was crying. It was very emotional."

Said Cindy: "And that's when the nurse called me back, and scheduled me to see the surgeon right away."

Test results showed Stage 3 inflammatory breast cancer, a rare and aggressive disease that does not offer a favorable prognosis. It progresses rapidly, often in a matter of weeks or months, and is difficult to diagnose before it is too late.

"We went home and he (Colen) makes all the phone calls to everybody," Cindy explained. "I start smoking a pack of cigarettes and drinking wine. I mean, I seriously thought, 'I'm dying.' I didn't know what to do. I was just numb, and I wasn't sure how to tell them, so I let him do it.

"I just sat there while he made the phone calls and smoked one after another, and drank. The only thing that was going through my mind was, 'Bury me in red.' I was already planning out my funeral. I did that for three days."

Colen added: "That was a tough night. I had to call her dad and her mom and her stepdad, her brother, and tell them. She was planning her funeral, picking out the clothes and all that."

While they waited for the following week's doctor appointment, the couple spent a lot of time on the Internet to learn more about the battle they were facing. What they found was not encouraging.

"What we're finding is pretty scary," Colen said. "We're finding that it says inflammatory breast cancer only appears in about three to five percent of cancer patients. It's a very rare cancer, and only about five percent of people who are diagnosed live for five years. Take that back, it was 18 percent live five years.

"The reason being that the cancer doesn't present itself in a way like other breast cancers. It's very hard to diagnose. Ninety-five percent of those cancers are Stage 4. Once you're Stage 4 with inflammatory breast cancer, it's a death sentence.

"I was just trying to be positive, and just doing as much research as you can. Trying to tell her she had to fight, but I didn't really have to tell her that. She already had that spirit."

Colen and Cindy met 24 years ago after both went through painful divorces, and Colen took a job as a bartender at a club in Harker Heights owned by Cindy's mother. One night they went out, and have been together pretty much ever since. They got married in February 1998 at the famed Little White Wedding Chapel in Las Vegas.

After the initial shock wore off, Cindy began to come to grips with her condition, but it was her first visit to the oncologist that convinced her there was a chance she would survive.

"He said, 'Cindy, I'm not going to treat you. I'm going to cure you.' That's the first thing he said to me. I said, 'OK.'

"I just felt like, 'I can do this.' I couldn't see myself passing away. I wasn't done yet. Every time I would see him, he was just so positive.

"Those first three days were really hard, but after that I just did what I had to do."

Her treatment included six months of chemotherapy, a double mastectomy, followed by six weeks of radiation.

Chemo treatments every three weeks were brutal, but Cindy continued to go to work as much as she was able.

"I remember the first day (of chemo), you're just sitting there and you don't really know what to expect. It's cold, and you can feel it going in. You're laying there with a blanket, and there are people around you who are getting sick and having to get blood transfusions.

"They were giving me instructions, and they said, 'When you go to the bathroom, you have to flush it twice.' It's so toxic, you have to flush twice. That was what was going through me.

"My hair started falling out in chunks. It was Easter, and my mom shaved my head, then my son shaved his, and we all took a picture.

"The main thing was being tired – I was tired all the time – and it's a tired where you can't sleep it off. I would start to put my pantyhose on, and I had to take a break. So it took me forever to do things, and right after my chemo treatment, my bones would hurt real bad.

"You would just get to feeling better, and then you would have to go through it again. Two to three days after a treatment, it hits you. Then you're down for a week, then you start to come back up, and it's time to do it all over.

"And then you have to worry about 10 years down the road, what the chemo has done to your body. It can start breaking down your heart and your lungs. That's what usually happens – people beat it (the cancer), but the chemo causes something else down the road.

"But I'll take 10, 12 years, compared to one."

When all those rounds of chemo were completed, it was time for major surgery. The first time she looked at herself in the mirror after the operation "wasn't pretty."

"Still today, I don't like to look in the mirror," Cindy says. "It's always a reminder. To be so young, you know. I felt like, at 37, I'm done. Everything I put together as being a woman was just gone.

"I remember walking up to Colen one time," she said, pausing as tears filled her eyes and choked her voice. "I said, 'If you want to leave me for somebody else, it's OK.' And he said, 'No, I'm not going anywhere.'"

"It was pretty devastating," Colen said. "Her breasts were beautiful. But I married the heart, not the body. I loved the body, but I married the heart."

Following radiation therapy, which was the worst part of the whole ordeal, Cindy had to wait a year for her body to heal before she could undergo reconstructive surgery. Then there were regular trips back to the doctor for checkups and blood work, every three months at first, then six months, and then once a year.

So far, the news has always been good – no evidence of cancer. It has been eight years, so she is beating the odds, but Cindy knows there are no guarantees.

"They don't tell you that you are cancer-free. My doctor says, 'I'll tell you a story. I had a lady that made it 10 years. But then it came back with a vengeance, and she didn't make it a year.' They thought she was cured, too, so he said, 'I will not tell you that you are cured.'

"He said, 'It can come back, even after 10-12 years, so if you get a cold that lasts longer than the average person, if you start getting a pain that's just not normal – you're not normal anymore – you go straight to the emergency room.'

"It's scary. I can go to pick up something, and if I get a pain, I have to think, 'Is it from doing that, or something else?' So you live with it every day.

"My message is to get tested. So many people – and men are the worst – ignore things. They don't go and get it checked out.

"And if something is wrong and you know it's wrong, keep fighting for it. Don't just take a doctor's word because they're a doctor. My doctor had no clue. Get a second opinion, or just keep pushing until you get what you want done. If I had taken those antibiotics, I wouldn't be here.

"If I had waited one more week, my oncologist said it would have been a different story."

Chapter Four

Route 66

A few days ago, I was standin' on the corner in Winslow, Arizona.

Not only that, I saw the "... girl, my Lord, in a flatbed Ford, slowin' down to take a look at me ..." that Glenn Frey of the Eagles sang about in the classic song, "Take It Easy."

See her?

I spent the night in Winslow as I drove along historic Route 66 from its origin in downtown Chicago to its finish at Santa Monica, in southern California. Also known as the Will Rogers Highway, the Mother Road, and the Main Street of America, U.S. Route 66 was established in November 1926 and became one of the most famous roads in the country, running a total of 2,448 miles through Illinois, Missouri, Kansas, Oklahoma, Texas, New Mexico, Arizona and California.

Route 66 was once the primary way people traveled across the country, before the massive interstate highway system was developed. I decided this would be my summer adventure.

Last week, after lots of beautiful, rugged scenery driving mostly interstate highway out of New Mexico and into Arizona – not all of Route 66 remains intact today – I rejoined the Mother Road and found myself heading into Winslow, and I had to stop and take a look at the famous corner immortalized in song by the Eagles.

I found out that the song was actually mostly written by Rock and Roll Hall of Fame member Jackson Browne. It seems Browne was having trouble finishing the song, and grudgingly handed it over to Frey, his upstairs neighbor in a Los Angeles apartment. Frey finished it and included the song on his band's first album released in 1972.

After I snapped a few photos at Standin' On The Corner Park

in downtown Winslow, I walked just across the street to Don and Sandra Myers' "On The Corner" T-shirt and souvenir shop and chatted them up. None of the Eagles band has ever stopped by their store, but two years ago, Jackson Browne himself walked through the door.

"He was standing right behind where you're standing now," Don said, a big grin on his face.

"It was so cool," Sandra added. "He came in with his girlfriend, bought a lot of T-shirts, and the next day he even did a little mini-concert with his whole band out in back of the La Posada Hotel. He played about 10 songs, and he told the story about how he wrote, 'Take It Easy.'

"He was headed back to California and his car broke down three times, once in Winslow. The last time it broke down was in Flagstaff, and he left it on the side of the road and never saw it again. His friends had come up behind him in a five-panel Dodge van, picked him up, heading back to L.A., and he wrote the song in the back of the van.

"He wasn't all the way done with it, and Glenn Frey kept hearing him working on the song. The Eagles were working on their first album, and Glenn Frey kept telling him, 'That's a great song. I need that song.' And he kept telling him, 'No, no.' Finally, he bugged him enough and Jackson Browne said, 'OK, you can finish it. But you have to put something in there about how the women out west drive pickup trucks, because it's so damn sexy.'

"He said Glenn Frey did the song the ultimate justice by putting in something about God, women and pickup trucks, all in one line."

Unlike many towns that thrived during the heyday of Route 66 and are now withering away or mostly extinct, downtown Winslow is coming back to life, thanks in no small part to Route 66, which passes right by the famous corner. The Myers say they get between 100 and 500 people a day —including visitors from all over the world — during the tourist season, which starts to die out every year in November.

"Winslow used to be the main hub of the railway in Arizona.

"When Route 66 came through, it put a big hurt on the railway. Then the interstate came through and killed Route 66 – that's a story everybody knows. It really destroyed this downtown," Sandra explained.

"But in the last 15 to 20 years, Route 66 has become what is saving this town, actually. We're still a railroad town – over 100 trains come through here a day, and 90 percent of the people are employed by the railroad. But Route 66 is revitalizing our downtown.

"Do you know how Route 66 was completed? Did you hear that story? When they started building Route 66, they ran out of money. That was around the time of Prohibition, and Al Capone needed a way to get his stuff to the west coast. He funded the finishing of Route 66. It's true."

After several days on the road, driving through America's heartland, meeting and talking to a variety of people along the way, I started becoming convinced that the historic highway is America's Pilgrimage.

There are a number of ancient expeditions around the world, including pilgrimages to the Holy Land in the Middle East, pilgrimages to Rome and the Vatican in Italy, and the 500-mile Camino de Santiago in Spain – which I have experienced three times, the first trek in 2011, again in 2013, and again in 2017.

I truly think that this is our historic pilgrimage. Not in the same religious or spiritual sense, of course, as the others, and the trip is accomplished by means of driving rather than walking, but there are a number of similarities.

There is vast history along Route 66, the same way there is incredible history along the Camino de Santiago, the only other pilgrimage I know anything about. Not nearly as much history, but some pretty cool history, nonetheless.

As I traveled Route 66, I used a guidebook to navigate, the same way I did on the Camino. The directions are confusing at times, and once in a while, you get lost – or at least think you may be lost; may have taken a wrong turn. Sometimes, your gut – your instincts – tell you that you're heading the wrong way, and you retrace your "steps," and find your way again. Sometimes, just as you're starting to seriously wonder if you've made a mistake, a sign appears along the path and lets you know that all is well.

The route passes through tiny towns that once were thriving, back in the old days when Route 66 was the featured course for folks headed west. Now, many of those towns are dying off, or trying desperately to hang on. Same thing on the Camino, with a network of small towns and villages, and people scraping together a living.

Just like on the Camino, for the most part, everyone you meet on Route 66 – both locals and fellow travelers – are warm and friendly, willing to sit and talk for a while with some knucklehead from Texas (me) who tells them he plans to write a book about it. One of those was Sal Lucero, a New Mexico native proud of his heritage and still working to preserve the history of Route 66 in tiny Moriarty, about 40 miles east of Albuquerque.

Lucero has lived for more than 40 years along Route 66 in Moriarty, beside the now-defunct Whiting Brothers service station – which he operated for 20 years – and the historic Sunset Motel. The station hasn't pumped gasoline since 2003, but he keeps it open as an historical site.

"Let me tell you something, when I took over this station, it was (busy) 24/7. You had to wait on line both sides of the road to get service.

"I quit selling gas in '03. You know why? They wanted new pumps; they wanted new gas tanks. They just won't leave you alone. I had an above-ground tank that was not leaking, but every day – two or three times a week – they were coming in here, bothering me. So finally, I said to heck with it. I stopped selling gas.

"I like to keep it open, because it's a historical place, you know. What would I do at home? My wife, she's gone. That's her, right there," he said, pointing to a large portrait of him and his wife, Inez, who died a little over a year ago at age 75. They were married 54 years.

Lucero – father of three, grandfather of four and great-grandfather of one with another on the way –would not admit to his own age, saying with a smile: "I'm as old as my little finger, sir. I don't talk about age. I'm up there, my man; I'm up there."

With that, Lucero stood up and abruptly cut off the interview. He and two friends were working on some tires when I arrived, and he wanted to get back to work. He shook my hand and wished me well, told me to enjoy Route 66, and I was on my way down the road.

Chapter Five

Heroes and comic books

Mike Reed loves comic books.

Characters like Superman, Batman, Thor, Aquaman, and The Flash take him back to a childhood that most people would want to forget, but Reed, a retired U.S. Army sergeant who served during the 1990-91 Gulf War in Iraq and saw combat during Operation Desert Storm, says he would not change a thing about the way he grew up.

"We never lived in the same place longer than six months, if we stayed that long," the 59-year-old Alabama native said. "I've got (seven) brothers and sisters that were born from Virginia to New Mexico. When my stepfather was around, he was drunk, knocked all of us around.

"I saw him beat my mother to death when I was 10 years old. I just finally decided … you've got to leave all that stuff behind you and go on. I can't change any of it."

After his mother's death, Reed, who has never known his biological father, was sent to live at the Alabama Free Will Baptist Children's Home in Eldridge, Ala. He stayed there from fourth grade through high school, until he joined the military when he was 19.

"I was in the reserves my senior year of high school," Reed explains. "I graduated on the 19th of May, and on the 20th of May, I was at Fort Jackson, S.C."

Thus began a long and successful career that included deployment to serve in the war with Iraq. By that time, he was a legal NCO in Fort Hood's 2nd Brigade, 1st Cavalry Division, doing the same type work as a civilian paralegal, or legal advisor.

He came home from the combat zone with a few problems he did not have when he left, including post-traumatic stress disorder

(PTSD) and the onset of tuberous sclerosis, a rare condition that causes benign tumors to grow on the skin, the brain, and various internal organs.

"I came back from Desert Storm (in 1991), and I was covered in these (small bumps on his skin). They say it's genetic, but I didn't have a problem until I came back," says Reed, who continues to undergo treatment for the disease.

"I still feel like I didn't have any problems until I came back from Desert Storm. I came back, and I was sick as a dog."

After he was medically retired in 1993, Reed was encouraged by his wife, Brenda, to pick up an old childhood passion for comic books. She hoped that would help get his mind off his own problems, and also keep him out of her hair.

"I was driving her crazy, and she said, 'You need to find something to do.' When I was a kid, comic books was a way of escaping."

Now, Reed has a tall bookshelf full of Marvel Masterworks and DC Archives editions that contain reprints of thousands and thousands of vintage comic books, dating back as far as 1936.

He has the first 90 issues of the Justice League, which includes such characters as Superman, Batman, Wonder Woman, The Flash, Green Lantern and Aquaman; the first 150 issues of The Avengers, which originally included Hank Pym, Hulk, Iron Man, Thor and the Wasp; the first 90 issues of The Fantastic Four; the first 175 issues of X-Men; all of the Legion of Super-Heroes (Superboy and Supergirl); and a lot more.

Reed says he prefers to collect the hardcover anthologies, instead of the more valuable paper comic books, because he enjoys spending time reading them.

"I like 'em like this because I can look at them. Some people have the actual comics, but they've got them in plastic wrap, and you can't look at them. For me, that's no good.

"One of the reasons I know about comics is because when I was a senior in high school, we all had to do a term paper, and I was given the assignment of comic books. Before that, where it started was from me wanting to read The Phantom (newspaper) comic strip. I didn't want anybody reading it to me – I wanted to read it myself."

Watching Reed sort through his collection and talk about the various superheroes is an interesting and educational way to spend an afternoon. I had no idea, for instance, that in the early days of his existence, Superman – who first appeared in a comic book in 1938 – did not fly. He could leap tall buildings in a single bound, and was faster than a locomotive, but it wasn't until much later that he acquired more powers, including the ability to fly and x-ray vision.

In the 1950s, Senate hearings were held to consider the negative effect of comic books on children. This came after the publication of psychologist Fredric Wertham's book, "Seduction of the Innocent," which suggested among other things that violence in comics was dangerous to young, developing minds.

"That killed all the comics except for Batman, Superman and Wonder Woman," Reed explained. "For 12 years, you could only get those three."

In 1954, the Comics Code Authority was formed by the Comics Magazine Association of America as a way to allow comic publishers to escape government regulation and self-govern the content of comic books in the United States. CCA members submitted their comics to the organization for approval prior to publication. If found acceptable, a special authorized seal was printed on the cover, allowing it to be sold.

This went on until the turn of the century, when newer publishers bypassed CCA. Marvel Comics abandoned the practice in 2001, with others following suit over the next decade, until the Code went out of existence.

Reed, meanwhile, says he prefers comics from the "Golden Age," when books were 64 pages long and sold for 10 cents. Today's comic books just do not compare.

"I like the older comics from the '60s and '70s, even the '80s. The artwork is much better today – I think because they use computers to draw with – but the stories were much better back then.

"Comic books, in general, were better back then. You pay more for them now, and you only get about 20 pages – ads and everything. You get less story, and they don't have the imagination they had back then. In my opinion, they're not worth it, but that's just my opinion."

Now living quietly on Copperas Cove's west side, Reed and his wife of 23 years, also an Army veteran, get by on monthly military retirement checks. His life hasn't been the easiest, but he considers himself fortunate and he has no regrets.

"My wife is the best thing that ever happened to me. The children's home was the second-best, and the Army was the third-best thing that ever happened to me.

"My brothers and sisters are bitter. They think the world owes them something. I don't talk to them – or they don't talk to me. The real reason is, they think I've got it made because I'm retired, and also because I don't have anything for them.

"I love them, don't get me wrong, (but) my kin people all told me I thought I was better than them. I said, 'Let me set you straight on something. I don't think I'm better; I know I am.'

"What I mean by that is … I'm not better than anybody else, but I'm as good as anybody else. I don't have to live the way they do. I don't think the world owes me anything.

"I go to church, and I try to live right. My wife says I talk a lot better than I used to. At one time, I'd cuss you out in a heartbeat, and if you wanted to fight, I'd knock you on your rear end. But I don't want to be like that anymore. I'm almost 60 years old, and that's a bad way to live.

"In the end, life's been good to me. I have a good life. I don't have anything to complain about. I wouldn't change my life, even if I could. I think people are crazy to talk about 'what could have been.'

"I've got a lot more to be thankful for than I do to complain about."

So, what do you think so far? Pretty good stuff, ain't it?

People are pretty good folks, for the most part, after all.

Well, keep reading, and if you're so inclined, head over to my website, www.johnhenryiii.com and say hello. You can also leave a review on Amazon and let people know how much you're liking this book. That's right – you don't have to wait until you're finished. Go ahead. It only takes a few minutes!

All right, back to the stories …

Chapter Six

Let's Ride

Never ask a Harley Davidson owner if you can ride their motorcycle; never leave a fellow biker stranded on the side of the road; and never, ever paint a Harley green.

Just a few rules of the road for motorcycle riders, according to longtime biker Paul "Hippie" Munsel, former owner of Cen Tex Customs service and repair shop.

"Younger people will laugh at you and say it's an old wives' tale," Munsel, 66, says. "But I know first-hand that a green Harley is bad luck.

"I painted one green one time for a friend of mine. My dad blew a gasket over it. He ranted and raved. A bunch of us took off on a little ride – about 80 miles each way – and on the way back, a drunk driver came across the road and took my friend out, right in the middle of everybody. Dad had told me bad things happen, and that kind of made me a believer."

Munsel, a native of Shelbyville, Ind., 26 miles southeast of Indianapolis, moved to Texas 40 years ago after a stint at Fort Hood and serving in Vietnam for a year with the U.S. Air Force. He lived in Johnson City and Austin, then a visit to Hearne in the Bryan-College Station area turned into a 35-year stay. That is also where he acquired the unique nickname.

"I went over there to help a buddy get a Chevrolet body shop re-opened," Munsel explained, sitting just inside the front door of his Avenue D shop, surrounded by motorcycles in various states of repair and re-assembly. "I figured I'd be there about six weeks – two months, at the most – and I needed a place to live while I was there.

"I went to talk to a guy about a rental house, and he said, 'I don't rent to no damn hippies.' My beard was down to here (halfway down his chest) and my hair was down my back. So I went back to work, and a couple of days later, that same guy called my buddy and said, 'You still got that damn hippie down there? Tell him to come on back down here. I might have a place for him.'

"That's how it got started, and it just stuck. You go over to Hearne and ask about Hippie, and they'll tell you anything you want to know. You ask about Paul, and they won't have any clue. I used to have people make checks out to Hippie, and I'd take 'em down to the bank and cash them. It was no big deal."

Twice divorced, father of four, Munsel was preparing to shut down his Hearne shop after 35 years in business to spend more time with his girlfriend, Becky, who was fighting advanced colon cancer. Things unexpectedly took a turn for the worse, and Becky died.

Munsel says his world turned upside down.

"The doc said it was in remission, and we were all excited and everything, but about two or three weeks later, she started hemorrhaging real bad. The cancer had never gone away. She had more surgery, and they gave her two years to live.

"In October 2013, she started going down pretty hard. She was a dispatcher for the sheriff's office. I lost her a year ago February, and I was having a hard time.

"When she passed away, I just didn't even want to wake up anymore. I had nothing else to look forward to, you know? My life was gone. When my second wife divorced me, that was real bad – we'd been together for 28 years. Becky and I had been together for two years, and we just fit together like hand and glove. It really hurt."

His two sons, one a retired firefighter, convinced Munsel to move to Copperas Cove, and he convinced them to start another motorcycle shop. For Munsel, turning wrenches on bikes is just what the doctor ordered.

"I was just as depressed over here as I was over there (in Hearne)," he said. 'Just sitting around doing nothing. We originally opened this up to be a family operation. This is really more for them than for me. When they decide they want to step in, they will decide on whatever share they want.

"We had to jump through a lot of hurdles, because of city

codes and (other) requirements, and that slowed us down. But now, we're good to go. We've had some ups and downs, but I think those are smoothing out. We're on a shoestring budget, but I've got a couple of good guys working for me, (and) I've got another part-time guy.

"I've got about 49 years' experience in doing motorcycles and customizing cars. We can do anything from changing the little cap on the valve stem to a full-blown build. We've had a real good reception in this town. We're doing pretty good."

The afternoon I stopped by the shop, it was so full of bikes that Munsel was working on one in his showroom, just inside the front door. Parked right behind that was his beloved black 1980 Sportster, temporarily out of commission with a broken piston and ring.

"I've had her for 18 years. We go everywhere together. She's just about back together, but all these others come first, then I get to take care of mine.

"I've been on motorcycles for a long time. Dad put me on a motorcycle when I was nine months old. He slept at Grandma's for about two weeks after that – that's about how long it took Mom to calm down," Munsel said, laughing. "I started working on my own at age 14, and I haven't stopped.

"The old guys like me, it's just a passion. You develop a better relationship with your Harley than you do with your wife, your girlfriend, or even your kids."

And whatever you do, never paint a Harley green.

"I built a bike for a guy and painted it a nice, bright yellow and put white pearl over it. It looked kind of like a lemon freeze, and he loved it. About a year later, he and a bunch of his buddies decided they wanted to start painting bikes, so they stripped his down and painted it a beautiful candy green. I told him, 'You shouldn't have done that.'

"About six months later, he found out his wife was pregnant, and then she lost her job. He lost his job, and then they repossessed the motorcycle. Then, a guy that I know ended up with the motorcycle. He pulled the tank off and brought it to me. He said,

'Here, you can have it.' I said, 'I don't want it. I know that tank.'

"He said, 'I don't have any use for it. Why don't you strip it down and paint it?' Well, I had the shop about a week, and man, everything was going wrong. I was losing money left and right. I couldn't figure out what was wrong. One day, I was getting some tools out and I looked over and saw that tank. I said, 'That's it.' So I called a friend up and said, 'Hey, come get this Harley tank – you're always looking for extra parts and stuff.' I told him the whole story, and he said, 'Yeah, I'll take it home.'

"He was a big four-wheeler fanatic, and after he took that tank home, he blew the engine up on one four-wheeler and wrecked two of 'em in about two weeks. He called me up and he says, 'Mr. Hippie, you're right. This tank is bad luck! I sanded it down and shot black primer on it.' I said, 'Did you strip it?' He said, 'Nope.' I said, 'You have to strip it.'

"Before it was all over, he took that tank down to the Brazos River, filled it full of rocks and sunk it."

Chapter Seven

Mama's birthday

My mother died June 15, 2000, and I still miss her all the time.

A few years ago, I interviewed one of Copperas Cove's sweet senior citizens for a story, and as we were talking, she mentioned that she would turn 79 years old later that month. I asked her which day, and when she told me the 23rd of April, I got goosebumps.

This lovely lady and my mama were born on the same day, same month, same year – 6,000 miles apart. One in Hungary; the other in California.

Early birthday wishes to both.

I only wish I could bake my mother a birthday cake and take it to her this weekend. I think she would have made a neat little ol' lady.

Mama was born Billie Jo Fern, daughter of George and Sybil Fern, younger sister of Virginia. Younger sister by just over 10 months.

Grandma might have kept cranking out those babies, too, except she had to undergo a partial hysterectomy and was not able to have any more.

Last Saturday, I called my Aunt Virginia, who lives now with one of her two sons down in League City, and asked her to share some memories from back in the day. With her own birthday coming up in June, Auntie V looks and acts a couple of decades younger than she really is, and it didn't take much prompting to start the story ball rolling.

"Every year between April 23 and June 6, we were the same age," she said. "People would see us and they would think we were twins. We'd say, 'No, we're just sisters.'

"They'd say, 'Well, how old are you?' And I'd say, 'Five,' or whatever. Billie would say she was five, and they'd say, 'Well, how come you're not twins?' We never could explain that, but we knew that my birthday was coming up and it was going to change.

"We looked so different. Our features were the same, but she had blonde curly hair, and I had black, straight hair. I looked like a little Mexican girl, and she was a pretty little blonde-headed thing.

"We didn't look like twins in any way, except mama made our clothes and she always dressed us alike."

The Fern family started out in San Pedro, Calif., where both girls were born, then moved to Texas, where my Paw Paw went to work as a quarantine inspector for ships arriving at ports along the Gulf coast.

"We lived in California until just before I turned four," Virginia said. "Daddy was a bigot, and he did not want his little white girls going to school with little black boys. So we moved to Texas. In the meantime, he got hired by the quarantine service, and we went to Sabine Pass (on the Texas-Louisiana border).

"I went to school through second grade there, and then we moved to Galveston, and we lived there until I was in the ninth grade, so Billie would have been in the eighth grade. After that, we moved to Houston in 1949."

While they were living in Sabine Pass, in a house with no indoor plumbing, the Japanese bombed Pearl Harbor and the United States went to war. I asked my grandmother one time what she remembered most from those days, and she said it was the difficulty she had getting enough sugar due to rationing.

Aunt Virginia remembers supporting the war effort by helping out with a government drive to collect rubber as part of a series of scrap-donation campaigns that also included such things as metal and newspapers.

"Billie and I each had a little rubber doll. We decided we were going to give them to the rubber drive. I think the purpose of the rubber drive was probably to make tires and stuff for the vehicles they were using in the war, so I don't know that our dolls were of any help with that, but we thought we were doing the right thing.

"I remember cutting my little doll's head in a 'X' so it would smash flat. Or, having daddy do it, probably. They kept telling us we didn't have to do it, but we did it anyway. We thought we were being patriotic, and helping the war effort.

"I remember when Pearl Harbor happened. Daddy had this old box wood trailer that he used to haul stuff. He was backing that trailer into the driveway down there in Sabine Pass, and that's when we heard about Pearl Harbor. It was horrible.

"We lived on a corner lot, in a house that had no plumbing. No bathroom. You had to walk out to an outhouse to use the bathroom. And we had to walk past the chicken coop or whatever, and there was a rooster out there that was mean as the devil. You had to carry a stick with you because he was going to get you.

"I hated going in that thing because it had those granddaddy long-leg spiders in there. But that's what you used.

"When we took a bath, we had a bucket that mama filled up with water on the back porch, and we all used the same water. When we moved to Galveston, we got plumbing.

"We didn't have TVs until the '50s. We didn't have a TV until we moved to Houston. Daddy bought Granny a TV, and he bought us one. They were round screens, and the picture was green.

"It's amazing how things have changed, just in my lifetime. I started out typing on an old manual typewriter. Now, of course, I use a computer."

Along with spankings that would be considered child abuse in today's world, the Fern girls learned other lessons the hard and painful way, as well.

"There was one way to do things, and it was George Fern's way," Virginia told me.

"I always loved tomatoes, and mama would slice them up and put them on the table. There was one slice left on the plate out in the middle of the table, and I reached out with my hand to get it, and daddy went to stick it with a fork, and got my hand instead.

"I'm crying because my hand's been stuck with a fork, and he's eating the tomato. I don't think he was purposely being mean … reaching out for food with your hand was not the way you were supposed to do it, and he showed me.

"I never did it again.

"He would send you outside to get a switch. If it wasn't big enough, he would go get one. I remember one spanking I got which was done with the wire end of a fly swatter. It was to the point blood ran down my legs. He'd get mad, and he'd just keep on.

"Pete (her son) tells me he can remember back when I'd spank my kids with a belt. He said, 'You'd hit us, and we'd act like it hurt, then as soon as you left the room, we'd all laugh.'"

There is a lot of longevity, good hair and bad teeth on my mother's side of the family. Unfortunately, her fate was to be stricken with something called a glioblastoma, which is a particularly nasty type of brain tumor. She never had a chance.

Aunt Virginia says she is blessed to have continuing good health, although she often wonders about the fairness of her sister's death.

"In my opinion, she was as close to perfect as you could be. I was always the one who did everything wrong. When she got sick at the last, I didn't understand why she was sick and dying, and I was still gonna live. It was amazing to me, and it still is.

"My health is extremely good, I think. When people see me and I tell them I'm going to be 80 in June, they say, 'Uh-uh, no way.' But it's the truth.

"I have high blood pressure, and I take four pills a day for that. I can't do all the things that I used to do, and I realize that, and I kinda sit and watch TV a lot – sometimes with my eyes closed," she said, laughing.

Here's to my mama and to my Auntie V.

Happy birthday, y'all.

Chapter Eight

Rattlesnake Roundup

Several years ago at the Oglesby Lions Club Rattlesnake Roundup, snake handler David Gay got in the way of a western diamondback strike that caught him just above the top of one of his cowboy boots.

That bite – he called it a "nick" – hurt like hell and made his leg swell up, but it was nothing compared to a vicious bite he suffered five years before that.

"One fang got through my pants leg, but it didn't require medical attention," Gay, a retired police officer from Taylor, said, as he helped corral dozens and dozens of snakes inside the live pit at the Oglesby Community Center, about 15 miles east of Gatesville, Texas.

"The doctor can't tell you anything. All they're going to tell you is it's gonna swell up and hurt. I knew that ahead of time, and I didn't need to owe anybody a bill for telling me what I already know."

One of his little fingers is permanently swollen from the effects of rattlesnake venom, and another bears a nasty scar that is a reminder of a bite that very nearly brought his snake-handling career – and his life – to an early end.

"That was a bad one," said Gay, who has been hospitalized three times for snake bites. "I flat-lined in the hospital on that one. I think I had a reaction to the anti-venom. I got six vials, then I flat-lined, and they had to bring me back. That was seven years ago.

"I retire every time something like that happens – for a year or so – then I come back."

This was the 47th annual rattlesnake roundup hosted by the Oglesby Lions Club, which contributes all profits from the event to a number of charities. Along with the snake hunt, there was a wide array of arts and crafts, food vendors, musical entertainment, car show, bike show, children's train rides and other attractions.

One menu item I had to try, of course, was some fried rattlesnake. I had never eaten rattlesnake and was looking forward to it. Well, either the pieces I got were overcooked, or it is an acquired taste. Fried shoe leather would have been easier to chew.

Bummer.

Oglesby Lions Club president Ray McEnroe – "Like the prima donna tennis player (John McEnroe), except you can look at me at 300 pounds, and tell I've never played tennis in my life." – said he is proud of the roundup, which attracts several thousand visitors to the town of about 400 people that he has called home for the past 30 years.

"We're not the biggest snake hunt, but I do believe we're the second-oldest," said McEnroe, a 56-year-old retired welder who was born in Marlin, has been married for 35 years, and is the proud father of three children and "a bunch" of grandkids.

"This event has been going on for 47 years consecutively. Locally, we do a lot of charities, scholarships for kids. We donate at the international level and the state level, which (supports) the state of Texas diabetes camp for children.

"People can go to a website called charitynavigator.com, and they will find that the Lions Club International has a 96-plus rating, and there's not a lot of charities that can claim that. We are required to be a non-profit, and that's what we do. We make the money and we give it away.

"I don't generally go into a whole lot of specifics. Gross (revenue) is one thing, and what we come away with is a whole lot different deal. But I imagine we made in the range of $15,000 (last year).

"We try to put on a good show, and make it affordable for people. I tell everybody a husband and wife and two kids can come in here with a fifty-dollar bill, and they can get in the door, take in a show; get something to eat. So many things cost so much money now, (but) you don't have to take out a loan to come here and have a good time."

People were flooding into the grounds surrounding the Community Center around mid-day Saturday, and it was standing-room-only around the snake pit.

Gay, who has been a rattlesnake handler for 30-35 years, said his fascination with the cold-blooded critters began when he was a kid growing up in Lexington, a small town about 50 miles northeast of Austin.

He used to hunt snakes, even after he was grown, but now he mostly leaves them alone, except for exhibitions and helping out with "nuisance removal," when someone finds a snake in and around their home or business.

"I got started when I was about that age," he said, pointing to a boy who appeared to be about eight years old, crouched on the floor near my feet, looking into the snake pit.

"We lived out in the country, had a lot of snakes around, and if you wanted something to play with, you went out and caught one. I don't remember the first one I ever caught, but I remember the first time I got into trouble with one.

"I brought a water moccasin into the kitchen. Had him in a bucket, and ruined a good dip net getting him in there. So, daddy had some choice words for me, as he was jumping up and down on the kitchen floor, killing him with a softball bat. Then, of course, mama had some choice words, as well. She said we needed to leave our snake killin' to the outside.

"I've always liked snakes, and I especially like rattlesnakes.

"They do a lot for the environment, and snake venom has uses in all phases of medical technology – things like clot buster drugs, for stroke victims, heart attack, some cancer killing agents. Mice are covered with ticks, so they probably help control some Lyme disease, and Rocky Mountain Spotted Fever, things like that.

"They do a lot for the environment, and of course we're removing a bunch of them from the environment (this weekend), but these are all western diamondbacks, and they're very common. There's about 30 varieties of rattlesnake, and about 10 of 'em you can find in Texas.

"Ninety-nine times out of a hundred, you see a rattlesnake, and it's this kind right here. You see the coon tail, the black and white rings right before the rattle? That's a western diamondback. They are 60 percent or more of all the rattlesnakes in Texas, so they're pretty much a renewable resource."

Gay, married for 30 years, father of two and grandfather of two, said he was not sure how many rattlers were rounded up this year, but one hunter he spoke to brought in around 300 pounds worth. The average western diamondback weighs two-and-a-half pounds, he said, but some can reach nearly six feet long and seven-and-a-half pounds.

"These will be sold to snake brokers, and they sell the meat, the hides, bones – they don't waste a thing. Some of them may go to venom research facilities."

His advice to anyone encountering a rattlesnake in the wild is simple – if you hear that unmistakeable buzzing sound of the rattle, the first and probably most important thing you can do is to stop.

Immediately.

"I try to let people know that they're not an attack animal,' Gay said. "I mean, you see a lot of these will strike at us, but there's a whole lot more that aren't. Nine times out of 10, you come up on a rattlesnake in the wild, and you're probably going to walk right past him.

"For every one you see, you probably already passed four or five. They basically strike for only two reasons: food and fear. We're too big to eat, so really the only time they will bite is when they feel threatened.

"If you hear a rattle, freeze. Get real still. They're not a lone animal. If there's one, there's going to be others. You want to look around and see if there's any other snakes with that one, locate a good escape route, and slowly move away in that direction.

"They don't want a confrontation any more than you do."

Chapter Nine

Talkin' Texan

It was another brutal evening football practice many moons ago down in the swamplands of my hometown Houston, Texas, when our sometimes sadistic coach gathered everyone around for a talk, and one of the young players promptly threw up all over his cleats.

"There you go, Lloyd!" coach roared, at the poor slobbering, crying, heaving, overweight, backup lineman. "I told you not to eat dinner before practice! There's your supper, Lloyd! I swear, boy, you're dumb enough to be twins!"

Not very nice, but that was this guy's way. He was tall and strong and loud, black horn rim eyeglasses, thick, curly black hair, bushy eyebrows, big Roman nose, and with a last name like Di Cristofaro, most likely of Italian descent, but some of the expressions he used – like "dumb enough to be twins," for example – were pure Texan.

Here are a few more fine examples of Texas speak:

Dumb as a box of rocks.

Dumb as a post.

Dumb as dirt.

Can't ride and chew at the same time.

If you put his brains in a bumblebee, it'd fly backwards.

Couldn't pour (water) out of a boot with a hole in the toe and the directions on the heel.

Dumb as a watermelon.

Dumb as a wagon wheel.

If his brains were leather, he couldn't saddle a flea.

If her brains were dynamite, she couldn't blow her nose.

Not enough sense to spit downwind.

He don't know diddly-squat.

The list goes on.

Here in the Lone Star State, we sometimes have a rather unique way of expression. Take the word "Howdy," for instance. This is an informal greeting, sort of a Texas 'hello' that evidently originated as a shortened form of "How do you do?" Native Americans reportedly used the words "how-do, how-do" as a greeting when addressing Anglo settlers back in the 1800s.

According to an article on pbs.org, the heritage of what some call Texas English goes way back to at least 1840, when people from the Upper South (North Carolina, Kentucky and Tennessee) started moving here in large numbers, along with folks from the Lower South (Alabama, Georgia, Louisiana, Mississippi, South Carolina). The complex mix of dialects from those places was even more complicated by an influx of European immigrants from such countries as Germany, Austria, Czechoslovakia, Italy and Poland.

Then, of course, there was the influence of settlers from Mexico, which has increased in recent years and will likely continue to grow.

Texas gained more population than any other state from April 2010 to July 2011, according to U.S. Census Bureau reports. The Lone Star State grew by an estimated 529,000 people during that time period, followed by California (438,000), Florida (256,000), Georgia (128,000), and North Carolina (121,000). The country's population as a whole increased by 2.8 million, to 311.6 million. California remained the most populous state at the end of that reporting period, with 37.7 million residents. Texas had 25.7 million, with New York at 19.5 million, Florida at 19.1 million and Illinois 12.9 million.

At the 2010 Census, the population in Texas was listed at 25,145,561, an increase of 20.6 percent from the 2000 count of 20,851,820.

The state's population hit an all-time high of 26,528,398 with 2013 estimates. Texas has three cities with populations more than one million: Dallas, Houston and San Antonio. There are six cities with populations over 500,000.

Contemplating all those numbers might be about as exciting as waiting for paint to dry, or eating a mashed-potato sandwich, but all the signs seem to point to Texas growing faster than a scalded cat or maybe a prairie fire with a tail wind, which could cause more problems than a big ol' hole in the fence, and means there is most likely fixin' to be a continuing evolution of our unique Texas English language, as more and more non-native Texans come here for the prosperity and glory about which we all love to boast.

For some people, all those newcomers crowding the highways and byways are about as welcome as a porcupine at a nudist colony. Or a skunk at a lawn party. As welcome as an outhouse breeze, or a tornado on a trail drive.

For others, the good times means Texas will remain in tall cotton, running with the big dogs, having more than we can say grace over, and being well off enough to eat fried chicken all week long. It is definitely better than being as poor as a lizard-eating cat, not having a pot to pee in or a window to throw it out of, having a tumbleweed as a pet, being too broke to pay attention, or so poor that even if a trip around the world cost a dollar, you couldn't make it to the Oklahoma line.

And boy howdy, it's no wonder all those people are moving here. Texas is a mighty fine place to be, with normally mild and short winters, but this year things have been a little different. Some might say it has been as cold as a well-digger's knee. Cold as a frosted frog; as an ex-wife's heart; a cast-iron commode; a mother-in-law's kiss; cold as hell with the furnace out.

People, including me, were enjoying the dickens out of last weekend's beautiful warm, sunny winter conditions. Clear blue skies, warm sunshine. And you'd better enjoy the nice weather while you can, folks, because when summer rolls around and kicks into high gear, it's going to be:

Hot as Hades.
Hot as a two-dollar pistol.
Hot as a billy goat in a pepper patch.
Hot as a pot of neck bones.
Hot enough to fry eggs on the sidewalk (sometimes literally).
Hotter than blue blazes.

Hotter than a fur coat in Marfa.

So hot the hens are laying hard-boiled eggs.

Even for native Texans, those who have lived here for decades, it is not easy dealing with 100-plus degree days that go on and on. Sometimes, the scorching heat can last for weeks at a time. There were 79 consecutive days over 100 in Laredo in 2009, surpassing the previous record of 42 days set by Dallas in 1980.

After a while, the relentless heat can make you as mean as a mama wasp. Mean enough to:

Steal the flowers off grandma's grave.

Beat somebody senseless and tell God they fell off a horse.

Steal the widow's ax.

Take mama's egg money.

Steal the nickels off a dead man's eyes.

I've lived in Texas all my life, and maybe I just fell off the turnip truck, but there's really no other place I'd rather be. It makes me feel lower than a gopher hole sometimes, and like I couldn't jump off a dime, when people talk badly about my state, but come hell or high water, you can sure bet the farm and take it to the bank that just because a chicken has wings don't mean it can fly.

And always remember, please don't ever forget:

A worm is the only animal that can't fall down.

Never sign anything by neon.

Keep your saddle oiled and your gun greased.

You can't get lard unless you boil the hog.

It ain't gonna get ironed if it's still hanging in the closet.

If you cut your own firewood, it'll warm you twice.

There's more than one way to break a dog from sucking eggs.

Give me the bacon without the sizzle.

Don't hang your wash on someone else's line.

Lick that calf again? (Say what?)

Why shear a pig?

Don't snap my garters.

A guilty fox hunts his own hole.

Quit hollerin' down the rain.

Don't rile the wagon master.

And last but definitely not least:

Better to keep your mouth shut and seem a fool, than to open it and remove all doubt.

Adios, y'all …

Chapter Ten

Makin' a Splash

Raul "Roy" Villaronga was so enamored the first time he laid eyes on his future wife, Julia Bush, he did what any young, red-blooded Puerto Rican male attracted to a pretty girl would do – he picked her up and tossed her fully dressed into a swimming pool.

"She was so (ticked) off," Villaronga said, smiling.

"I was furious," Julia agreed.

It was during a between-semesters trip to Houston from Texas A&M University in College Station, where former Killeen mayor Villaronga was in his freshman year as an engineering student and member of the famed Corps of Cadets, when the couple first met through a mutual friend.

The occasion was Julia's 16th birthday celebration. She was friendly with Villaronga's buddy, who had invited him to the party, and even fixed him up with a blind date. At some point, Villaronga asked his friend if there was anything they could do to help make the event more special.

"He said, 'Well, it wouldn't be a bad idea to throw her in the pool.' That sounded like a good idea, so I met her, introduced myself, and in the midst of the celebrations, I picked her up and threw her in."

After helping young Julia up and out of the water, Villaronga went looking for her parents, found them, introduced himself, and made a rather surprising announcement.

"I went inside and I said, 'Who are Julia's parents?' The Bushes introduced themselves, and I said, 'I'm Raul Villaronga. I'm from Puerto Rico. I'm a freshman at A&M, and I think I want to marry your daughter.'"

Julia was not impressed.

"I thought he was the most egotistical person I'd ever met," she said.

Villaronga doesn't think so.

"I say that she was smitten," he said. "I know I was impressed with her. She was a fiery gal. I thought she was something special. That was my freshman year; we got married my senior year. I guess it took four years for her to decide I wasn't such a bad guy after all.

"I'm not sorry I did it. Things have worked out pretty good. Like everybody else, we have had our differences and problems, but we have always been able to work them out, and we're happily married."

Indeed. The couple is celebrating 57 years of wedded bliss later this month. They have three sons, three grandchildren and a great-grandchild.

Roy and Julia recently returned from an extended road trip over to Nashville, Tenn., and then back through Baton Rouge, La., to watch their beloved Aggies play football against Vanderbilt and LSU. They have been season ticket holders since 1983, and gone to countless games since then, both at home and away.

"It's fun," Villaronga, 77, says. "That's our vacation. I'm fortunate to have a wife who likes football, and likes to travel. We both enjoy getting in the motor home and getting away. It's a vacation for the two of us. We both cook, clean up, work together, and it works out pretty good."

The road to becoming a die-hard Aggie – aren't all Aggies die-hard? – began down in Ponce, Puerto Rico, a United States territory of 3.6 million people in the northeastern Caribbean, where Villaronga was born and raised in a family of three children. His father was an accountant, and his mother a school teacher and housewife. He graduated from high school in 1954, and promptly followed a dream of moving to the U.S. and studying to become an engineer.

"My high school counselor's son was a senior at A&M when I was a senior in high school," Villaronga said. "I told him I wanted to study engineering, and I wanted to come to the States.

"Every recommendation he gave me, it always ended with – 'and my son is graduating as a civil engineer from Texas A&M.' So, uh, I think I was suckered into that one," he said, with a grin.

It was rough-going at first, becoming acclimated to a new culture and to the rigors of college life and military-style discipline, but Villaronga graduated in 1959, got his officers' commission a year later, and joined the U.S. Army. Lessons learned at A&M helped forge a successful military career that lasted 26 years, and saw Villaronga build an impressive resume that included serving with the 7th Special Forces Group (Airborne) at Fort Bragg, N.C., followed by two tours in Vietnam with the 8th Cavalry Regiment (Airborne).

He came home and was promoted to major, and eventually to colonel before he retired from the military on Aug. 1, 1985.

Villaronga went to work as a part-time professor at Killeen's Central Texas College, and later as a Department of Defense consultant, and then with the state Child Support Enforcement Division. Although he was working in Austin, his home base was in Killeen and Villaronga got interested in local politics. He ran for City Council in 1989, served a two-year term, then ran successfully for mayor in 1992, becoming the first person from Puerto Rico to be elected mayor of a Texas city.

At age 77, he remains active in a variety of civic organizations, including Veterans of Foreign Wars, American Legion, Disabled American Veterans, League of United Latin American Citizens, and National Association for the Advancement of Colored People. He and Julia both serve on the board of directors for Killeen Crime Stoppers, and are members of the Greater Killeen Chamber of Commerce.

With his extensive military background and training that includes a number of awards and decorations, including a Silver Star, Legion of Merit, Meritorious Service Medal, Air Medal, Joint Service Commendation Medal, Army Commendation Medal, National Defense Service Medal, Vietnam Services Medal, Armed Forces Reserve Medal, Army Service Ribbon, Army Overseas Service Ribbon, Vietnam Cross of Gallantry, Vietnam Campaign Medal, Combat Infantrymen Badge and Master Parachutist Badge, Villaronga has his opinions on how to solve the many problems facing the United States today, including the spread worldwide of terrorism.

The need for military might is an unfortunate reality in defeating enemies and keeping the peace, he says, and he has no doubt there is a military solution. But perhaps equally as important as bombs and boots on the ground is a unified front back home rallying behind any and all combat campaigns.

"Sure, there's an answer – there's an answer to everything," Villaronga said. "I don't think our Lord would put something on us that we can't resolve. But we've got to take a deep look at ourselves.

"Right now, I feel about the same way I did when I was a captain in Vietnam. When I went back for my second tour, we had a tremendous problem with drugs and morale. The people here in the United States did not support it (the war), and I saw the division in how our nation worked, and it was very depressing.

"Jump forward, and take a look at today. There's absolutely no respect given to the president of the United States. I don't care if you disagree with him politically, you should support and respect the office.

"I think we are destroying our own fiber, as a nation. To me, the biggest issue right now is, we have forgotten how to work together as a country. And I think that does more damage than anything else.

"I think a military solution is there, sure, but a military solution will not work until we also have a civil solution in our nation. As long as we're fighting among each other, I think everything that is happening with ISIS right now is just political fodder.

"We have an enemy, and I think a lot of people are taking advantage of that and fomenting a lot of hate, and a lot of fear, as a means of accomplishing what they want.

"Until we, as a nation, learn to work within the system, we're going to continue to have problems. I don't care who gets elected … well, yes I do … but once the election is over, it is our duty to work with whoever is elected to make our nation great. Whoever is elected should receive the support and allegiance of all the people in this country.

"Some of the best times we have had in our nation are when Democrats and Republicans worked together. They don't give up their ideology, they just put it down and put the mission, the objective, above their partisan objective.

"We don't have that right now, and it is sad. It is very, very sad. I think we need to grow up, and mature.

"Let's use our military the way it should be used. But there is nothing more demoralizing for a soldier than to look back home, and see that people are divided and fighting against each other.

"We need to show some support and some resolve to the people we send to fight our battles, by working together for what is best for our country. Until we do, our military operations are not going to be successful."

Chapter Eleven

90 years strong

Myrtle Hummer is a survivor.

Growing up on the family farm during the Great Depression, Hummer worked in the fields near the Texas-Louisiana border picking cotton, corn, peas and peanuts before school and after school – sometimes instead of school – to help feed a household that included eight kids.

It was that learned toughness, perhaps, that later helped the Evans, La., native endure the loss of two of her children, most of her brothers and sisters, her husband of 50-plus years, not to mention a series of heart attacks and frightening strokes.

"If you get your choice, take the heart attack," Hummer said, laughing. "Strokes are a whole lot scarier than heart attacks."

A resident of Copperas Cove, Texas, for the past six decades, Hummer was preparing to celebrate her 90th birthday with a celebration from 1 to 3 p.m. at Robertson Avenue Baptist Church. The church hall will likely be filled with friends and family, but no gifts.

"It ain't gonna be no party," Hummer says, flatly. "It's just coffee and cake, punch and tea."

Sitting at the dining table in her neat ground-floor apartment, Hummer – who says the only bad thing about turning 90 is the frustrating gaps at times in her memory – recalled moving to Copperas Cove, next door to the massive Fort Hood military post, when she was about 30 years old.

She was born and raised in Evans, a small farming community with two small grocery stores, a cemetery, two churches and a school near the Sabine River that separates Texas and Louisiana. The family raised various crops and livestock, and so escaped a lot of the hardship caused by the devastating nationwide Depression.

Hummer remembers community hog-killings after the first cold spell when she was a girl, and syrup-making time, when the sugar cane crops were ready.

"We were lucky. We had the farm, and we raised all of our own food. It wasn't a hard life – I didn't think it was. I was used to it. We were a lot more fortunate than people who lived in the cities."

She graduated from high school in 1941 and got married that same year. Her husband, Thurman, served with the U.S. Marines during World War II, and the couple eventually had four children.

I asked my Grandma Sybil many years ago what she remembered most about life during the Second World War, and she said it was the trouble she had getting sugar, which was rationed, along with such things as gasoline, tires, meat, shoes.

Hummer agreed.

"And coffee," she said. "You couldn't get sugar, and you couldn't get coffee. I was from Louisiana and we was used to drinking a lot of coffee. So what we did, we would take mine and his (Thurman's) pound of coffee, then we'd buy two pounds of chicory, and mix it all up together. We were used to drinking strong coffee, and it wasn't bad at all."

Around the time she turned 30, and her youngest daughter was five years old, Thurman took a job as a sanitation engineer on Fort Hood and the couple moved to Copperas Cove. There wasn't much here at that time, and they had a little trouble finding a place to live after they arrived.

"When we come here, there was no houses. We were very lucky to find a rent house. There was three little houses ... you know where Mickan's service station used to be? There was three little two-bedroom houses there, and we rented the middle one.

"The next year, we built a house on Turner Street, which was one street over, back toward town. So I raised my (four) children in that house, right back of the Robertson Avenue Baptist Church."

After the kids were grown and out of the house, the couple started traveling and lived for a while on Toledo Bend Reservoir, a 185,000-acre man-made lake on the Sabine River, back near their Louisiana roots. They had to give up living on the lake after

Thurman lost one and then both legs to complications from diabetes.

"He had already lost one leg when we first moved down there, and then whenever he lost the second leg, that's when we sold the house down there and moved back here. I just told him, well, we just have to change our lives, our lifestyle."

Thurman, who started the Copperas Cove Veterans of Foreign Wars post shortly after moving here, also suffered a debilitating stroke and died 23 years ago at age 70 from heart and kidney failure.

Myrtle, meanwhile, has had her own share of health scares, including three heart attacks and three strokes. She uses a walker to get around her apartment now, and no longer allows herself to drive a car.

"My stroke was such a creepy thing. The first two were TIAs (Transient Ischemic Attack, or mini-stroke) which are just warnings. But the third one, my left side was paralyzed for about three-and-a-half months. The only good thing was that I did not lose my speech.

"According to my son, Jerry, I slurred my words. I could not tell I was slurring, but he said I was.

"When it happened, Jerry was living by himself at Pidcoke and I was living by myself in a house I owned in Copperas Cove, and he called to check on me that day. We talked for a while, and he said, 'Mother, I'm going to come stay the night with you.' I said, 'Well, good, but you don't have to. I'm doing all right.' He said, 'No, mother, you're slurring your words.'

"So he came and was spending the night, and I got up to go to the bathroom. I had a TV against the wall, and as I started across the room, I started to fall and I couldn't stop myself. I crashed right into that television set. I called for Jerry, but he didn't wake up, so I crawled over to where I had a desk and a chair – I knew the chair had a metal bottom on it – and I found some kind of a stick and started banging on the bottom of that chair. That woke Jerry up and he came running in there and found me.

"He said, 'What's the matter?' I'm sitting there in the middle of the floor, and I said, 'I don't know. I can't get up.' "

Jerry was diagnosed with cancer in 2008 and died two months

later when he was 63 years old. Her youngest daughter, Gail, was killed in a car accident at age 19. All her siblings are gone, except her youngest brother, who lives in Evans and has an 82nd birthday coming up next month.

She has a daughter, Gwen, who lives in Tolar, two hours north of Copperas Cove near Stephenville, and her oldest child, Wayne, lives in Granbury, not far from Tolar. She has nine grandchildren and "more than that in great-grandchildren."

Hummer, who remains active with the VFW Ladies Auxiliary, has suffered a lot of pain, heartache and loss during her 90 years, but she is matter-of-fact about it all, saying "that's just life." Neither she nor Thurman ever felt sorry for themselves, she says.

"If you were around us for very long, you'd see that whatever God sends, we take it. I can't say we're very religious, but I guess you'd say we were brought up to be religious.

"We traveled all over the country. The first weekend after they let him (Thurman) out of the hospital from losing his second leg, we went to Dallas and they put those controls on the steering wheel, and he drove to Toledo Bend that same day.

"One thing I never had to worry about was my husband always kept a job. We didn't have a lot of money … for years, we didn't have insurance like they have now. We always had to make sure we kept a little bank account in case one of our kids got hurt or something like that, which they did. You planned for these things, (because) you knew they were going to happen.

"I think it's just the way I was raised. We knew that if we lived, we was going to die. It doesn't make any difference how much money you have or anything like that, when it is time for you to die, you are going to die."

Chapter Twelve

Soul of an artist

A young person struggling to find his or her way in the world is not an unusual thing, but when that someone is also harboring a deep, dark secret that could turn their world upside down, the degree of difficulty can increase exponentially.

Just ask Angelo Gomez.

A 50-something-year-old artist and musician born in Snyder and raised in the Midland-Odessa area of west Texas, Gomez is comfortable now with the direction he has taken, and the lifestyle he leads.

Such was not always the case.

"I was a junior at Midland High, (and) we got transferred to Brownfield, south of Lubbock, where the credits didn't transfer and I ended up being a junior again, at a new high school. I just said, no, I don't want to do this. So I dropped out. It was a very tough time in my life, and I ended up just leaving. I wanted to follow my dreams as a musician.

"I was a little freak in high school – hung out in the smokers' corner, wore jeans and concert T-shirts, had kinda longish hair. I never played any sports. I tried to get on the swim team at Midland High, and I was a complete failure. I just wanted to be a rock and roller. Music was all I had.

"I went through a lot of heartache and a lot of adjusting, coming into being Angelo Gomez. It wasn't until I went to college some years later that I really discovered myself as a person, and realized who I was. I had a really big epiphany at that time.

"Most of it had to do with my sexuality, probably. I had to accept the fact that I was gay, and that was a big, major turnabout for me, my family, everybody."

Along with getting his general equivalency high school diploma, and graduating from Midwestern State University in Wichita Falls at age 27 with a degree in arts and sciences, Gomez went full-speed ahead in his quest to find success as a rock musician.

He played in various bands throughout Texas, and shared stages with the likes of Rob Halford of Judas Priest, and Philip Anselmo and the late Dimebag Darrell of Pantera fame. His bands, including one called Ariel, opened for those heavy metal icons, until his musical tastes took him in a different direction.

"I wound up quitting all that, because … the heavy metal scene was something I loved, and still very much do, but I started getting into more collegiate music – REM, Jeff Buckley. We played at a club that was called 724 A.D., which was a really historical, popular club and destination for a lot of famous bands."

Gomez moved to Austin, but never gained a foothold in the music scene there, so he headed north, back to Wichita Falls for a while, then found himself moving out west to Alpine, Texas, near Marfa, home to a world-famous art community. That is where he discovered a passion for painting.

"That's where I woke up as an artist," Gomez said. "I saw the light. That's where I started realizing I am an artist and I am a musician."

Sometime later, he moved to Dallas, met his longtime partner, Mark, and continued painting, mostly abstract acrylics. It was tough going, and he was forced to take a series of day jobs to make ends meet, while trying unsuccessfully to make it as an artist.

Eventually, he wound up in Temple, where his mother lives, and found a music and art scene that lacked energy and support. So he decided to try and do something to liven things up.

A few years ago, Gomez – who plays keyboards, bass guitar, and sings – founded the Art and Music Visions of Central Texas Collective, a growing group of music and art lovers from throughout the region. Follow the group on Facebook and you'll be privy to a wide variety of events designed to promote local artists and musicians.

"I also wanted to do this in Dallas, but it seemed like I would just get lost in the whirlwind there," said Gomez, who has since gone on to promote successful art shows in and around the Metroplex area.

"I thought, 'Why don't we have one here in Temple-Belton-Killeen-Copperas Cove?' I started realizing that we have the largest (military) base in the world; we've got colleges; we're right on I-35. We've got Southwestern University in Georgetown; we have UMHB; we've got Baylor (University) right up the road.

"With all that, I wondered, 'Why don't we have a big art scene here?'

"I saw a really awesome art scene in Xenia, Ohio, a small town. It was just flourishing. And I thought, 'Why don't we do this here?'

"I've had a lot of opposition, but I know what I'm doing is real, and nobody can really stop me."

His big dream is to establish a major art and live music extravaganza along the lines of Austin's South by Southwest festival. Last June, Gomez hosted the first Central Texas Art, Music, and Film Sensorium along the shores of Lake Belton, near Interstate 35, halfway between Austin and Waco.

Things are slowly coming together, he says, and will work out in due time. Maybe not as quickly as he would like, but he is confident about seeing his dreams come true.

"I would like to see a unified art scene, which I think we have gotten.

"There are some unspoken goals, but I don't really say, 'By this time, I want to have this,'' or 'By this time, I want this to happen.' I just don't believe in time at all. I never wear a watch. I live for the now.

"I can't help but think of the world as being ... there really is just one day. The sun – the one day – circles the Earth constantly. There's never two or three days, four days, two months. It's all just one time. So to me, there is no time to have anything done by, unless I've got a doctor appointment, or I have to deal with people who deal with time.

"I don't know if I'll be here tomorrow, or the next day. So I've got to live right now.

"I just want people to join me and help get this festival going. I want this festival (to happen) at least twice a year. Let's make something happen here.

"What we don't see enough of is people going out to support things like art and live music," said Gomez, who admires artists like David Hoyle, an actor, painter, and performance artist based in Manchester, England. "Go out and find an artist and a band – one of each – follow them, take pictures, post pictures. Be a groupie. Support them. Take your friends.

"People complain, 'Oh, there's nothing going on in places like Temple, Texas.' That's a bunch of bulls—t. There's a lot going on, but nobody goes. Everybody just wants to stay home.

"I think it's everybody's duty, who is into art and music, to go out and support an artist or a musician. I challenge people to do that."

Chapter Thirteen

Building smiles

Georgia native and longtime central Texas resident Jim Butler has three kids, six grandchildren and seven great-grandchildren, so he knows a thing or two about wiping away tears and turning a frown upside down.

For more than a decade now, the retired U.S. Army soldier and Vietnam War veteran also has been putting smiles on countless other little faces all over town and beyond, albeit in a somewhat unusual way.

More often than not, when Butler spies an unhappy youngster at the department store or in the grocery aisle, or some other place, he tries to inspire at least a grin. If a warm smile and a kind word don't do the trick, the 81-year-old turns to a nearly sure-fire method of spreading sunshine.

He goes back out to his pickup, retrieves one of the miniature wooden chairs he carefully handcrafts in his backyard workshop, and presents it to the temperamental tyke.

Works every time.

Well, almost.

"You get all kinds of different responses," Butler explained, relaxing on his back porch the day after New Year's. "Some people look at you (like you're crazy).

"One time, I went into Walmart, and this little girl was sitting in there, in a buggy, and she didn't look very happy. I asked her, 'I'll go out there and get this little chair, if you'll sit in it.' She kind of looked at me, you know, and never did really answer.

"When I went and got the chair and brought it to her, she didn't want to have nothing to do with it," he said, smiling.

"I said, 'You don't want it?' She said, 'Nope.'

"She was just big enough to talk good, you know. Little bitty thing. I thought, well, that's the first time I ever had that response."

Butler, who first came to Copperas Cove by way of Fort Hood in 1958, was born in Elberton, Ga., near the South Carolina border, and grew up in a family of three boys and one girl that traveled all over the south and three times out to California as their father, a general contractor who specialized in building houses, followed employment opportunities, including during World War II.

"The only thing that kept him out of the Army was he had four kids," Butler recalls. "They didn't want to draft people with that many children. He got his draft notice one time, but they didn't take him.

"I tell you what … you've heard about church mice being poor? We were right along with them. One time, we lived in a tent. Somewhere up around Virginia. I was probably about five or six.

"One thing it'll teach you is to be thrifty. I've always been very frugal, and my wife (Paula) is the same way, but we're trying to get out of that (habit). I just had another birthday, and I ain't got too many more years left to spend money."

Along with how to squeeze a nickel, another thing Butler learned as a boy was all the ins and outs of carpentry from working with his dad, who knew how to build every part of a house, from the foundation to the roof.

"We did the whole nine yards, except for the plumbing," Butler says.

After he graduated high school, he decided to go to business college and become a bookkeeper. Pretty soon, he got tired of crunching numbers and went back to sawing two-by-fours and hammering nails with the old man back home in Georgia, then one day as he was eating lunch, he spotted a couple of buddies walking with an Army recruiter.

"This place had six hamburgers for a dollar. I could eat six hamburgers in a heartbeat back in those days. So, I'm sitting there eating hamburgers, and I looked across the street to where the police station was, and two of my buddies come out of there with an Army guy.

"I said, 'What are you guys doing?'

"They said, 'Oh, we joined the Army.'

"I had been in the National Guard for two years by then – I think I joined to get enough money to buy myself a car – and I had no intention of joining the Army. But it wasn't a little bit later that I said, 'You know what? I'll go with you.' So I went home and packed a bag, and my mother was asking me what I was doing. I didn't say anything until I was finished packing, and then I said, 'I joined the Army.'

"She liked to have a wall-eyed fit."

That was 1955, and Butler was 19 years old.

After basic training, he spent nearly a year in language school in Monterrey, Calif., studying Hungarian, then he was assigned to a mountaintop listening post in Germany, monitoring radio traffic during the Hungarian uprising of 1956, when citizens began resisting the Russian occupation that followed WWII.

He later was stationed in Japan, served in Korea, and worked as a first sergeant in charge of a wheeled-vehicle maintenance company in Vietnam (1968-69).

It was while he was stationed in Germany that he met and married a pretty local girl named Paula – nearly 59 years ago.

"We met on a double date," Paula explained. "I had a boyfriend with me, and he had a girlfriend with him. But we decided that we liked each other better. Been together ever since."

As he listened to his wife describe that initial meeting, Jim threw back his head and started laughing.

"What happened was, I called her later and asked for that other girl's telephone number, and she said she didn't know what it was. So I said, 'Well, do you want to go out?'"

Paula smiled.

"That's right. I forgot about that."

When the Army first sent the young couple to Fort Hood, they lived in a small, one-bedroom house that still stands behind the 7-Eleven store on FM 116. Copperas Cove's population then was around a thousand people, and a two-lane highway ran between the town and the military installation.

A decade later, it wasn't much bigger.

"When we bought this house in 1970 (on 27th Street), there was nothing up there (to the west)," Butler said. "We used to sit right here and you could look between this house and over that way, and see horses walking up and down."

After he retired from the military at Fort Hood with 22 years' service, Butler worked as an auto mechanic and service manager. Now, he spends a lot of time out back of the house, tending to a nice-sized vegetable garden, and doing lots of woodworking.

He likes to keep busy, but says the years are starting to take their toll a little bit. He doesn't worry too much about getting older, and says it is things like building those chairs and giving them out to kids that helps keep him going.

"Oh, I've got some little health problems, but I stay active. I don't sit down too much, unless I have to.

"Day before yesterday, I built one of those picnic tables, and then I cut another one out and sanded it. By the time I finished that day, I think I was wore to a nub.

"I can still do what I want to do – it just takes me longer.

"I was born before margarine was, you know. Margarine used to be white, when it first come out. It came in a little cellophane bag, and there was a little capsule in it. If you wanted it to look (yellow) like butter, you mashed the capsule, and then you kneaded the bag.

"I get a kick out of the little kids, and building these chairs is just something I enjoy doing. I've got a great-granddaughter that's 16 years old, and I started building those little chairs when she was two years old.

"I made two little chairs and a table, and they're still in use."

Unlike that trip to Walmart, when the little girl rejected his offer of a brand new, handmade chair, Butler found a willing recipient last month during a trip to Killeen.

"We walked into Aldi's to go grocery shopping, and all of a sudden this little baby – I forgot what her name was – she showed up there, and she was lookin' a little sour. I tried to get her to talk, and she wasn't having any of it.

"So I said, 'I know what'll fix you right up,' and I went out and got one of those little chairs. When I brought it back, she still really wouldn't have nothing to do with it. She did sit in it one time, but her mom said that when she got it home, if she wasn't sitting in it, she was dragging it around. That was her chair.

"So, she liked it, and that made me feel pretty good."

Chapter Fourteen

Honor and sacrifice

Two heart attacks, prostate cancer, diabetes, bladder failure, and crippling respiratory problems are among the staggering litany of health issues suffered by Charlie Duren, a veteran of World War II, Korea and Vietnam, but the 90-year-old, wheelchair-bound New York native considers himself lucky.

"What you've got to realize is that a lot of guys are a helluva lot worse off than I am," Duren says. "I've got it made in the shade."

Born and raised mostly in New Rochelle, N.Y., just north of Manhattan, Duren grew up with two sisters, the son of a New York City cab driver. He went to Catholic school, but dropped out in 1944, his sophomore year, to join the war effort.

"All my buddies were gone," he explained, sitting in the living room of his tidy house in Copperas Cove, Texas, not far from Fort Hood. "I was the last of the Mohicans. I wanted to join the Army, but my dad said, no, you're going to join the Navy."

So he did.

After basic training in Idaho, Duren headed to Washington to join his battleship, the USS North Carolina, which set sail for Europe in April 1944.

"I hated every day of it," Duren said, of his three years in the Navy. "Things were good, (and) they paid me good, but you're out there in the middle of the ocean."

After the war was over and his hitch was up, he got married, moved to Omaha, Neb., and went to work for Omaha Cold Storage. Then, his wife got seriously ill, lost a baby, and medical bills started piling up, so Duren decided to re-join the military in 1948.

This time, he went Army.

Initially, Duren was assigned to Fort Campbell, Ky., and later joined the famed 1st Cavalry Division, one of the most decorated combat units in the U.S. Army, in 1949. A year later, he was shipped off to Korea for his second round of combat duty.

It was there that he experienced his second brush with sudden death.

The first near-miss was back in his Navy days, when the young sailor was on deck as the ship struggled in rough seas and he was nearly washed overboard.

"The ship was going like this (up and down, up and down), and I was on the deck," Duren said, motioning with his hands. "All of a sudden, the deck is up here, and I'm down here. I'm scooting across that deck, and I saw a line and I grabbed it and held on. After everything settled down, here comes the chief, and he says, 'I want to show you something.'

"He said, 'You see that hatch?'

"I said, 'Yes.'

"He said, 'That's what saved your ass.'"

The rope Duren had grabbed snagged on the handle of one of the deck hatches, preventing him from a certain trip overboard.

"Another time," he explained, "this was in Korea – it was hot, and I was digging my foxhole. I took my helmet off, and the first sergeant says, 'Corporal, put your helmet back on.' I reached down to get my helmet and a bullet whistled right over my head. I mean it was that close.

"Don't tell me there ain't nobody up there lookin' after you."

Two years after he came home from his 1950-51 tenure in the Korean War, Duren's first wife died from cancer, and he "bounced around" for five or so years before meeting an attractive redhead during a night out while he was stationed in Germany.

"What happened was, my whole family – except my mom and me – knew him, because I didn't associate with soldiers," explained Elizabeth, Duren's wife of 56 years. The couple has two children, two grandchildren, two great-grandchildren and a third on the way.

"One evening, (they) wanted me to go out, and I said, no. I worked 10 hours a day, and I wanted to stay home. But I went, and we met. We danced, and that was it."

The couple got married that same year, in 1960, stayed in

Germany for two-and-a-half years, went to California for nine months, then transferred to Fort Bliss, Texas, in El Paso.

In 1967, Duren was shipped off to Vietnam, for his third combat tour. It was there, where he worked as a radar technician, that he began to suffer a majority of his serious health problems, mostly due to exposure to Agent Orange, a powerful – and highly toxic – herbicide and defoliant used by the U.S. military to clear land and destroy enemy crops.

Unfortunately, Agent Orange was also found to have created serious health problems, including such things as cancer, nerve, digestive, skin, and respiratory disorders.

Duren was one of thousands who suffered.

"I sent my husband off to the war as a healthy man," Elizabeth said. "He came back completely changed. He was a sick puppy. One sickness after the other.

"He lost a lot of weight. He was very quiet for a long time. Now, there are places to go everywhere to get help. We didn't have that back then. It took me years to understand why he was so nervous, or jumpy, hollering at night, bumping me around, cussin' me out. I did not know, because he didn't talk to me about it."

While he was still serving in Vietnam, Duren suffered a heart attack, and was relegated to desk duty. He almost got a ticket home as a result, but turned it down.

"I got dizzy, but that was about it," he says, describing when the attack occurred.

"They were going to ship me home, but I said, 'No, you don't.' That was not the way I wanted to get out of there. I wanted to get out on my own two feet. So they took me off the radar, and I did paper work."

Elizabeth remembers that time as a terrifying three days back home.

"When he had his heart attack in Vietnam … my mail came in the afternoon. My friend's mail – her husband was in the same company as my husband – her mail came early in the morning.

"About 10 o'clock in the morning one day, she came to me, and I looked at her and said, 'What's wrong?' She said, 'Your husband got killed.'

"What do you say in a moment like that?

"That day, I didn't get no mail. But something in the back of my head told me, no. If my husband was killed, there would be somebody knocking on my door. I was trained on that already. So I didn't believe it. You have to realize that I grew up in Germany during World War II. I was a teenager then, but I knew what was going on. So I just did not believe it was true.

"Three days later, I got a whole bunch of mail (from him)."

Duren came home to Fort Bliss in 1968, and retired from the Army a year later as a sergeant first-class with 22 years' service.

A week after he retired, Duren went to work for eight years as a driver for an armored car company, then he and Elizabeth moved west to Washington, where they both worked for an electronics manufacturing company. As time went on, and health problems continued to mount, the couple decided to move to the Fort Hood area, where they could be closer to increasingly important military health care services.

"We had no military facilities in our area," Elizabeth explained. "We had to go all the way to Fort Lewis, which was a long way for us. I didn't want to go back to El Paso, so we decided to move to Fort Hood.

"That was 22 years ago, and we're glad we did."

Charlie agrees.

"We've gotten the best medical treatment we've ever had."

While he is most always confined to his wheelchair – he takes short walks through the house, and still drives a car sometimes – Duren says life is good, and he has no regrets, no complaints.

"What happened over there in Vietnam … if I was younger, I'd go again," he says. "I take 13 pills a day – the only reason I'm alive is because of the pills.

"I've got a lot of books that I read. I've got my (crossword) puzzles, stuff like that. I used to be into trains. That one room back there was full of trains, at one time.

"I feel fine. I'm good. Overall, I feel fine."

Elizabeth, who spends most of her time taking care of her old soldier, says she wouldn't have it any other way.

"I have him; I keep him," she said, smiling. "As long as the dear Lord lets me have him. That's all I can say."

Chapter Fifteen

Big Babies

OK, I'm man enough to admit it.

There are not too many things that really scare me. I'm not real fond of snakes; a police car on the side of the highway when I'm doing 80 mph makes me nervous; my wife scares me a little sometimes; but I have been told that I am a fairly courageous sort of fellow, because I've faced and conquered a number of fears in my lifetime.

It is said that bravery is not a matter of being unafraid. Instead, bravery is being afraid, and doing it anyway.

I've done things that would be considered brave, I guess: climbing on the back of a not-too-happy rodeo practice bull when I had no idea what I was doing and tying my hand to its back; riding a motorcycle 100-plus miles per hour down a narrow two-lane country road; traveling overseas by myself for the first time to walk 500 miles across a foreign country with nothing but a backpack; standing in front of a classroom full of teenagers. Things like that.

But there is one thing that always brings me to my knees. One thing that turns me from a grown man into a little boy.

Getting sick.

Last Thursday morning when I got out of bed, I knew right away something was not quite right. Usually, when a major illness of some sort is brewing inside, I'll feel a disturbance in the back of my head, sort of at the base of my neck. A drop in the barometric pressure inside my skull that portends an approaching storm. When that happens, I know it's not going to be good. This time, it didn't feel exactly like that, but there was definitely some turbulence going on more toward the front, up around the back of the eyeballs region.

I made it to work, but as soon as I got there, I knew I was in trouble, so I stuck it out for a few hours and then headed home at noon. By then, my head and chest were starting to heat up, and I was coughing and sputtering, wheezing and gasping.

Mama ... I don't feel good.

The next three-and-a-half days were spent either in bed or bundled up on the couch, swilling Nyquil and popping various cold and flu medications. Come Monday, I felt halfway back to normal and survived the day at work, and by that evening was starting to feel like I might be on the road to recovery.

I was pretty darn sick there for a while, sicker than I've been in a few years, but truth be told, it can take a heckuva lot less to put me down for the count. A routine case of the sniffles is more than enough sometimes to have me reaching for my pillow and blanket.

And I know I'm not the only one. As a matter of fact, according to a recent study, there are a whole lot of us sickness sissies out there.

To our credit, though, it is not our fault. I repeat – not our fault. I know; I know. In today's world, nothing is anybody's fault. However, in this case, there is actual scientific proof, fellas, that so-called "man flu" actually does exist.

In an article posted on www.inquisitr.com, Dr. Amanda Ellison, a neurologist at Durham University, says that when men get sick, they really do feel worse than women do when they get sick. When we say we feel terrible at the first sign of a fever, we really do feel terrible.

This is because men have more "temperature receptors" in the brain, Dr. Ellison explains, which causes us to experience symptoms more acutely. Such differences occur in the brain's hypothalamus, which regulates a variety of mechanisms including temperature. The hypothalamus in male and female brains is the same size during childhood, until puberty strikes, and the accompanying onslaught of testosterone causes the male hypothalamus to grow larger, according to the doctor.

"When you have a cold, one of the things that happens is you get an increase in temperature to fight off the bugs," Ellison is quoted in the article. "The bugs can't survive at higher temperatures.

When your immune system is under attack, the preoptic nucleus increases temperature to kill off the bugs.

"But men have more temperature receptors because that area of the brain is bigger in men than women. So men run a higher temperature and feel rougher – and if they complain (that) they feel rough, then maybe they're right."

Aha! I knew it.

But wait. There is more. Along with a physical explanation, there also may be underlying psychological factors.

Information posted on www.webmd.com indicates that researchers at the University of Glasgow studied nearly 1,700 people and discovered that men were far more likely to exaggerate their common cold symptoms than women. According to this report, researchers said men and women may have "different thresholds for perceiving and reporting symptoms, rather than actual differences in symptoms."

In other words, their symptoms might be the same, but males and females respond differently to those same symptoms.

William Schaffner, MD, chairman of preventive medicine at Vanderbilt University School of Medicine, agreed, saying there is nothing in medical literature to support any difference in male and female colds, but men are less likely to seek medical attention when they get sick. Also, men are generally not as inclined to outwardly express things like feelings and emotions, and this could cause them to seek a little extra tender-loving care when they start to slide under the weather.

"Men are less in touch with their feelings," said Jean Berko Gleason, PhD, professor emerita of Psychology at Boston University. "So it might be more difficult for them to interpret what's going on when they are overwhelmed or sick."

Gleason said that common societal expectations could exacerbate the problem, as well.

"Women aren't supposed to fall apart when they have a cold. So men who are needing some nurturing might take advantage of that on occasions when they aren't feeling well, to get some care and love from the people around them.

"In general, (though), the differences between the sexes are less than we think. We admire everybody who is brave, but the social pressures on men and boys are much greater."

Exactly.

Social pressures. Pressures at work. Pressures at home. Bulging hypothalamus glands.

Not only that, differences in the male and female immune systems may play a role in guys getting and feeling sicker than gals. A 2014 study published in the Proceedings of the National Academy of Sciences concluded that testosterone apparently weakens the immune response in men, according to an article found on the website, www.everydayhealth.com.

The study claimed that high testosterone levels in men resulted in a lower immune response to influenza vaccinations. Women and men with low testosterone levels had more active immune responses to vaccination that did men with higher testosterone levels.

"This is the first study to correlate poor immune response to testosterone levels in men," reported Mark Davis, PhD, the study's senior researcher and a professor of microbiology and immunology at Stanford School of Medicine.

So there you go.

Physical, psychological and hormonal proof. We ain't making it up, ladies. We're just men, and sometimes we don't feel too good.

Now, there are things a man can do to help offset these deficiencies. Not much can be done about that oversized hypothalamus and the overabundance of temperature receptors in the brain, but along with that extra little bit of TLC I know you're going to throw his way the next time the man of the house is feeling poorly, you can also, er, um, encourage him – AFTER he starts to feel a little better – to take up some of these recommended immunity-boosting habits, including finding ways to reduce stress and get more sleep:

Don't smoke.

Eat more fruits, vegetables, whole grains.

Maintain a healthy body weight.

Exercise.

Moderate alcohol consumption.

Regular medical checkups.

As far as the psychological need for comfort and nurturing that stems from his reluctance to share emotions and feelings … well, good luck with that.

Be well, y'all.

Chapter Sixteen

Documenting history

Growing up the daughter of Jewish parents who survived the Nazi Holocaust during World War II had a profound impact on Naomi Rosen's life that continues today.

The first American-born member of her family, 60-year-old Naomi spent a majority of her childhood in Queens, N.Y. Her late father, Isaac Rosen, who died at age 86, came to the U.S. in 1950, while her mother, Eugenia, arrived here in 1947-48, and still lives in Florida.

"My mother was born in '36. Her mother was in the Polish Underground (State). She had to leave my mother at a convent, where the nuns were hiding the Jewish children," Naomi said. "She had to learn how to call her mom, 'aunt.' Otherwise, it would be known that she is not an orphan.

"When he was deported, my father came from a village outside of Warsaw. It was an orthodox Jewish community. When he got to Auschwitz, somebody said to him when he got off the train, 'Say you are 16, not 14. Otherwise, you'll be killed, as one of the children.'

"He never saw his father again. Don't know where he ended up ... probably gassed. He and his mom were reunited after the war."

Her childhood in New York was difficult, Naomi says, as she was plagued with perplexing emotional outbursts and hyperactivity. By the time she reached age 14, her parents had run out of answers, and decided to send her to live in Israel, where she attended an agricultural high school for three years.

"At the time, it was the best thing for my ... disposition. My temperament.

"I was hyper-emotional. Heavy-duty emotional. I couldn't be what they all wanted me to be. It was so confusing, because you don't know who to please, and if you don't have your self-confidence yet, then what happens?

"Being brought up by European parents is very different from being brought up by American parents," she explained. "Their fears were very different than the fears of the American parent.

"In fourth grade, I was told to watch a program that had to do with the Holocaust. It was a Hebrew day school, and I was supposed to watch it for an assignment. My mother wouldn't let me watch it. I was the only one in the class who couldn't watch it. There were other children in the class with Holocaust-survivor parents, but basically, the bottom line was to protect (me) from their pain.

"I just couldn't behave like a European child was supposed to behave. I couldn't be what they had dreamt their freedom would bring, or something. I couldn't sit still that long. I was a wild kid.

"They kept dragging me to doctors, because they didn't know what was wrong with me. Every single doctor said, 'She's a classic bi-polar.' That really bothered me, because as time went on and I learned more about it, the biggest concern I had – even though my emotions were absolutely honest and real – was trepidation and questions about whether what I had to offer would be considered legitimate, because of how people are confused about what that's about.

"I was the black sheep. That was basically why I ended up where I ended up. I felt like I had let them down, but at the same time, I couldn't lie to myself. I mean, you can only wear high heels for so long.

"I absolutely loved Israel. I was a little cow-milker. I felt like I was productive, (and) I had a lot to offer. I was a good worker. I was a very good worker, but I couldn't stick to rules."

She returned to Queens when she was 17, moved across the East River to Manhattan a few months later, and got married. That union was short-lived, and Naomi, who always had a love and talent for drawing and painting, decided she wanted to become a potter, so she headed off to Italy to learn to make pottery.

After that, she moved back to Israel, where she lived on a

kibbutz, basically an agriculture-based Israeli commune where members lived and worked together for the common good. She was happy and content there for a while, then headed over to England, where she lived near Wigan, home of the legendary Wigan Pier, made famous by author George Orwell in his book, <u>The Road to Wigan Pier</u>. There, she continued drawing, painting with water colors and learning about English pottery.

Her back-and-forth world travels continued over the years, until she met Bob Emrich, a retired U.S. Army soldier to whom she has been married for 17 years. The couple has lived in Copperas Cove since 2005.

"I didn't know where home was – that's really it. I didn't know where home was," Naomi said last week, relaxing at the dining table, overlooking her shaded backyard. "I didn't understand myself (enough) to understand where I really fit.

"I always lived on the outside, except in the kibbutz. I was happy there, in a collective sense. When I came back to America, I thought I would be able to recreate that in downtown Brooklyn, but they were a little bit too political left-wing for me, and I ended up leaving the country again to go do pottery.

"I think it had to do with emotional confusion, and now that I'm older, I think it (also) had to do with the manic depression. That's what I really think."

She still suffers from depression now, but has mostly learned to manage it. One thing that helps her stay on an even keel, she says, is her painting. A member of the Five Hills Art Guild and participant in last month's Body of Art Five Hills Art Festival, she has a nice little studio at the house, which is filled in all directions with colorful canvases, large and small, dozens hanging in various rooms, down the hallway, stacked against walls, behind the bed, and in corners.

These days, her work is more than a labor of love or a creative outlet – the images she captures with her brushes come from deep inside, as a way of dealing with the emotionally painful turmoil she sees going on more and more around the world.

A beautiful painting currently underway is inspired by the recent terrorist attacks in Paris and in Brussels.

"I just feel like I have a responsibility to document these things," Naomi says. "There are so many things going on right now, (and) what am I doing about it? People from my family couldn't do anything during Hitler. What can I do about the things going on now?

"In this one, it's not giving any particular symbolism, but it's giving the emotion from it. "I don't know the title yet, but it is specifically being created since Easter with what happened in Brussels and in Paris.

"Sometimes I just watch it (an image) arrive. I stand there with the brush, and there it is. That's what happened with that painting. I don't actually see it; I move with it. Something gets in there.

"Everything is emotionally motivated, (and) the thinking comes later – hopefully, as little as possible. It's all emotional, really.

"The pieces that I'm preparing now are very serious, especially with this being an election year. I'm very nervous for this country, and for other countries – very nervous. I speak with some people, and I'll ask them if they are scared or nervous about this year; who do we vote for?

"But I find it is harder and harder for me to talk with people about politics. I don't want to drive them crazy, because it nags at me so often. It's hard to talk with a lot of people about serious stuff, so I paint.

"Thank God my husband knows so much history, because he helps me keep my emotions in check. The truth is, I am truly happiest when I'm working.

"I keep envisioning all these places where there are people (suffering), no different than any time in history. I feel the best place I can do something is documenting.

"Will it serve a purpose? I hope so. If somebody chooses to look at (my work), I guess I've accomplished my mission."

Chapter Seventeen

On a mission

Knocking on strange doors and asking people for a few minutes of their time to talk about God, sin, and salvation is not something for the faint of heart.

Sometimes, the results are encouraging, even entertaining.

Other times, not so much.

"One time, we knock on a door and a lady answers, and all of a sudden, we just felt all our happiness disappear," explained Elder Robert Mohrmann, a Mormon missionary working in Copperas Cove, Texas. "Just ... gone. It was like, 'We need to get out of here; we need to get out of here now.'

"She was smiling, with these really big eyes, but something just felt really, really wrong. So we left as fast as we could: 'Here's a pamphlet. Bye.'

"The moment we left that house, everything came back. That good feeling we had when we first got there. Everything was OK again.

"Another story ... this one didn't happen to me, but it happened to some other missionaries. They knocked on this door, and this little kid opened up, and he was like, 'Mom, the cops are here!'

"They hear the back door slam and they see this guy running for the nearest set of trees."

Mohrmann, 20, from Nampa, Idaho, and Alex Bower, an 18-year-old resident of Fort Mill, S.C., are serving two-year missions in Texas for the Church of Jesus Christ of Latter Day Saints, headquartered in Salt Lake City, Utah. Both were raised in the church, and shortly after graduating high school, they joined an estimated 30,000 young Mormons who volunteer each year for various mission trip assignments around the world.

They receive a modest stipend from the church missionary program, along with an apartment, but are responsible for funding the bulk of the cost of their 24 months of service.

"We don't get paid while we're out here; we pretty much pay to be out here," Mohrmann said. "We get $135 a month, so that's why we rely on (church) members so much for food.

"People are so kind – that's one thing I love about Texas: 'It's hot – you guys want some water?' 'Yes, please, thank you.'"

So what makes a young person basically take a vow of poverty and move across the country for two years to try and deliver a message that people mostly don't care to hear?

"The main reason I went on a mission is because I love heavenly father and I love Jesus Christ, and I know that's what they want me to do," said Bower, a tall, slim, soft-spoken native of Wisconsin who moved with his family to South Carolina at age six.

"I know they exist, and that's why I'm here."

Mohrman, who is nearing the end of his mission commitment and serves as a trainer and mentor for his new partner, is the more outgoing of the pair, and his explanation was slightly more involved.

"My story is a little bit longer," he said, smiling.

"When I was 12, turning 13, I went less active from the church for a while. I didn't have any friends there, I didn't know what I was doing there, so I thought, 'What's the point?'

"I felt like an outcast – my whole life, I had always been an outcast – but I'm going to church, going to all these scouting events, nobody is talking to me ... so I just quit going. Eventually, this one kid noticed that I wasn't coming to church as often, he expressed concern, and I thought, "Oh, you mean somebody actually does care? Well, let's see how much he actually does care.'

"So I went back to church. He sat next to me and talked to me, and we became best friends. In fact, he's serving his mission now in Brisbane, Australia.

"But I still didn't know (whether) the church was true. I was just coming because now I had a friend. Over time ... I started going over to his house and spending time with his family. I started seeing how he interacted with his family – which was way different than how I interacted with my family – how they had a different spirit about them, (and) how they were happy, and enjoyed being together.

"I decided, 'I kinda want this.' But how do I do it?

"I started praying a little bit, reading the Book of Mormon a little bit. And things started getting better – school was going a lot better. I was becoming less of an outcast. Then, when I was 17, I went on a thing called Trek ... which is where the youth go on a little adventure, like pioneers."

Alex chimed in:

"It's like three or four days where you go out with a bunch of the youth in your area, and dress up like pioneers and push handcarts ... to try and experience the same kinds of things they did."

"Ours was five days," Mohrmann continued, "and, oh my goodness. It was in the middle of June (in Idaho), and the first day was freakin' hot. I was dying. I'm a sweater – Texas kills me. But I'm feeling better about things. A lot of things were going on in my mind.

"I'm doing some service, which heals the soul, really. It helps a lot. Like, a young woman would come over and ask me, 'Hey, can you set up our tent?' I'm sitting there exhausted, because I have been the one pulling the cart all day, and my friends are telling me, 'Dude, you've got to learn to say, no.'

"Then, after Trek, I met this girl. We started talking and started liking each other, and she ended up helping me learn more about the gospel and having the desire to go on a mission.

"I was going to join the Marines. Over time, throughout my senior year, she wound up helping me decide to join the police force, instead. So, I decided to go on a mission and then become a police officer. On Trek, I was able to help people, make them happy, and I thought maybe I could do that a little more on a mission."

Both young men are Eagle scouts, no small accomplishment, and spend their days – after morning rituals that include 30 minutes of exercise, one hour of personal Bible study, and another hour of mutual Bible study — on a non-stop schedule of activity, including such things as community service at the public library, visiting with church members, and of course, the traditional door-to-door proselytizing.

Walking up to people on the street and asking them if they "know" Jesus is something Mohrmann has gotten used to, but he remembers the fear factor a newcomer like his partner experiences.

"So far, I haven't been doing a lot of actually going out and finding people," says Bower, who comes from a family of one brother and five sisters. "It's just been mainly teaching people who are interested. It's not too bad.

"When the fear starts to come in, I like to think about what Will Smith said in that movie, which is 'Fear is a choice.' It talks about that in the scriptures, as well — faith can overcome that fear — and it's definitely true. I'm not the super-outgoing type, but if you have faith in Jesus Christ ... he went out and talked to people, and people despised him and killed him. So the more that they reject me, the more I'm just becoming like him, so ..."

Mohrmann added:

"I'm been doing this for 19 months, and it has changed me a lot.

"The biggest thing is that I have learned how to love people. Before, I didn't trust anyone. I still struggle with trusting people, but I love them now. Here I am, going up talking to some random person, and I feel a genuine love for them. I know I have something that can help them be happy.

"So you have the fear of going up and talking to someone, but that's where fear and faith comes in. I have faith, so I'm going to talk to this person, and if they reject it, then, oh well. I did my part. I love them and I want them to have this."

When his mission is finished, Mohrmann plans to return to Idaho and join law enforcement. Bower's post-mission plan includes attending Brigham Young University in Utah to study computer science, then heading back to South Carolina to work with his father, a computer programmer.

Meanwhile, keep an eye out for these two young men in short-sleeved white shirts and ties. They very well may be heading to a neighborhood near you soon.

"I'm sure you know that missionaries get rejected – a lot – and sometimes very harshly," Mohrmann said. "Sometimes, you'll knock on a door and you hear the door lock. CLICK. You're like, 'Really?'

"We knocked on a door one time and we hear, 'No one's home!'

"Usually, we just talk to them for a few minutes. Give them something – most of the time, it's a Book of Mormon. We tell them, 'This is something we want you to read and pray about. We know it's true; we've tested it for ourselves. We're not going to make you do anything; we just want you to give it a shot.' Then, we ask if we can come back the next week.

"No matter how many doors get slammed in my face, I believe in what I'm doing, so I'm going to keep on doing it."

Chapter Eighteen

Texas Heat

"Summer's here and the time is right, for dancin' in the streets …"

Apologies to one of Motown Records' signature songs first recorded in 1964 by Martha and the Vandellas, but summer is here all right, and it is way too hot for this ol' boy to do any kind of dancing in the streets.

I have lived in Texas all my life, and I never get used to the scorching heat waves that invariably settle in during the summer.

Does it really get this hot every year?

Shoot, the other day it was so bad, I pulled a couple potatoes out of the ground in my garden and all we had to do to get ready for supper was cut them open, scrunch up the ends, add butter, salt, pepper and a spoonful of sour cream. Good eatin'. Pre-baked potatoes.

Not really – in fact, I don't even have a garden – but goodness gracious, it's hot out there. I was in Arizona a few weeks ago and they said on the radio that it was 111 degrees. It was pretty warm, but not like this.

Tuesday morning, I went in to wash my face and brush my teeth, turned on the faucet and the cold water tap burned my hands! OK, not really … but it is absolutely true that the coins I keep in my pickup console were nearly hot enough for a first-degree burn when I fished some out to buy a cold drink at the convenience store, and I'm really, really glad I put some of that air conditioner recharging stuff in about a month ago and the truck is blowing cool air again.

Wow, just now I looked out the window and saw two squirrels in the yard, crouched in the shade at the base of a large live oak tree, pouring blue Gatorade on each other. Not only that, the poor tree was whistling at the neighbor's golden retriever, trying to get it to come over.

And the bad news is, we have yet to hit our hottest stretch. According to The Old Farmer's Almanac, here is what's coming up in Texas:

Aug. 1-12: scattered thunderstorms, hot; Aug. 13-20: thunderstorms, then sunny, cooler north, scattered thunderstorms, hot south; Aug. 21-26: a few thunderstorms, seasonable (whatever that means); Aug. 27-31: sunny, hot.

Definition of hot? 100-plus degrees.

For you newcomers – and us oldcomers, too – the good news is it will start to cool off around October. Fall is arguably the best season in good ol' Texas, by the way. Winter temperatures, precipitation and snowfall will all be below normal across the state, with the coldest periods occurring in mid- and late December, and January.

In the meantime, here are some unique things experienced Texans know about their summers:

- The best parking place is determined by shade instead of distance.
- You break a sweat the instant you step outside at 7:30 in the morning before work.
- You can make instant sun tea.
- The birds have to use potholders to pull worms out of the ground.
- You can get sunburn through your car window.
- Farmers are feeding their chickens crushed ice to keep them from laying hardboiled eggs.
- You learn that a seat belt makes a pretty good branding iron.
- You discover that in July it takes only two fingers to drive your car.
- Cows are giving evaporated milk.
- You realize that asphalt has a liquid state.
- No one would dream of not having air conditioning.

Hey, you know some of those are true. And now for more good news. It's not as hot as it could be.

On June 28, 1944, in Monahans, Texas, near Midland/Odessa, temperatures reached 120 degrees, one day after Tipton, Okla., recorded the same scorching high.

According to accuweather.com, the highest temperature ever recorded not only in the United States, but the entire Western Hemisphere, was 134 degrees on July 10, 1913 in Death Valley, Calif. That was also one of five consecutive days when Death Valley recorded a high of 129 degrees or higher, and is the second-hottest temperature ever measured in the world.

Holding the dubious distinction of world record-holder is El Azizia, Lybia, where it was 136 degrees on Sept. 13, 1922.

While a high of 134 degrees is extreme even by Death Valley's standards, blazing heat is not uncommon there. The maximum average high temperature in July is 120 degrees, compared to the 106 degrees in Phoenix, Ariz.

In Lake Havasu City, Ariz., it was 128 degrees on June 29, 1994. On June 27 that year, Lakewood, N.M., reached 122 degrees. Fort Yukon, Alaska, had 100-degree heat on June 27, 1915, and Ozark, Ark., recorded a high of 120 degrees on Aug. 10, 1936, during the historic North American heat wave, which killed more than 5,000 people and devastated enormous numbers of crops as the country also endured the hardships of the Great Depression and the infamous Dust Bowl.

Known as the most severe heat wave in the modern history of the continent, the 1936 disaster began in late June when temperatures across the U.S. climbed above 100 degrees. Extreme drought conditions spread and the sweltering weather stretched into Canada.

Things peaked in July when North Dakota, Ohio, Texas, Oklahoma, Kansas, Arkansas, Minnesota, Michigan, North Dakota, South Dakota, Pennsylvania, Louisiana, Nebraska, Wisconsin, West Virginia and New Jersey experienced record high temperatures, along with the Canadian provinces of Ontario and Manitoba.

During a time when air conditioning was in the early stages of development and was mostly absent from houses and commercial buildings, many people suffered heat stroke and heat exhaustion, especially in high density population areas like Chicago, Detroit, St. Louis, Cleveland, Toronto.

According to farmersalmanac.com, people in New York City were "packed like sardines" at Coney Island, trying to escape the 106-degree heat, with residents in a number of Midwestern cities sleeping outside – on their lawns and in public parks – in an effort to beat the heat.

North America finally cooled down in September of that year, as temperatures and precipitation returned to normal, but the cruel summer of 1936 was one unforgotten for many years.

So there you go. One thing you can always count on here is the onset of stifling summer heat. It happens every year, and it never gets any easier.

If it's too hot for you, here's a suggestion: take a long walk off a short pier. Go jump in the lake! We've got two of the finest freshwater reservoirs in the state with Lake Belton and Stillhouse Hollow. Over in Belton, you can find Summer Fun Water Park, and up the road in Waco, Hawaiian Falls Water Park is a cool – no pun intended – place to splish and splash.

Take a trip to the Gulf of Mexico, which provides a number of options along the Texas coast, including Galveston Island, Surfside, Matagorda, Corpus Christi, Padre Island, Port Aransas.

Closer to home, Austin has a variety of beautiful swimming holes, including my favorite, Barton Springs Pool at Zilker Park. The three-acre pool is spring-fed and the water is always a chilly 68-70 degrees. A shock to the system when you first get in, but wonderful on a hot summer day.

Schlitterbahn has a water park in not-too-far-away New Braunfels, as well as in Galveston, Corpus Christi and South Padre Island.

New Braunfels is also home to the beautiful Guadalupe and Comal rivers, where you can canoe and float the day away on inner tubes.

There are lots of other ways to beat the heat, as well. One that I particularly enjoy is grabbing an ice cold beverage, stretching out on the couch, ceiling fan whirling overhead, watching a good movie or some sports on TV.

Ah, yes, life is good. Hey, honey, bring me another one?

Chapter Nineteen

Angels among us

Andrea Meeks and her kid sister, Drew, believe in angels.

"Absolutely," Andrea said. "Everybody has people around them to help them – your grandmother, your mother, your father. I get visits all the time from my mom, my dad, lots of people ... we never really die; we just change."

The Meeks girls grew up in the 1960s and '70s in Gatesville with their father, Dean, a well-known dairy farmer who played college football for legendary coach Paul "Bear" Bryant at Texas A&M and once attempted a solo sailing trip across the Atlantic Ocean, and their mother, Margaret. Both adored their easy-going dad, but often "butted heads" with their strong-willed mom.

"Nothing was ever good enough for her," Drew says. "And I also didn't always hear things right. If mom said it was black, I heard it was white. So we argued a lot."

The relationship between mother and daughters continued to be a challenge, even after the girls were grown and gone. In fact, it wasn't until Drew was in her early 40s that she began to see a different side of her mom.

"We were going on a cruise in February 2003, and I invited my sister," Drew explained. "I had bought four tickets ... I had separated from my husband, and I thought maybe he would come back. I was praying that would all work out.

"I had bought four tickets, two for Andrea and her husband, and two for myself and my husband. Well, her husband didn't like to be on a boat, and my husband didn't come back. I had given one of the tickets away to a lady that I knew, and Andrea and I decided we would give the other ticket to mom.

"I said, 'She's got to room with you,' and Andrea said, sure, no problem. So we go on the cruise, and we have a great time.

"When we got back, I asked my mom if she had a good time, and she said, 'Oh, it was all right.' And so once again, I had that (thought) that nothing I do is good enough. I was telling my friend how upset I was, and she told me that maybe I should ask God to start showing me my mother as he sees her.

"So I did. I started praying, and one day I was talking to my mom at a wedding, and my mom was going on and on about how my sister didn't take her girls to church and blah, blah, blah. So I made a smart-aleck comment, and I said, 'Mama, your mom must have drug you to church every Sunday.'

"She got real quiet, and she said, 'No. I wasn't allowed to go to church. And when I did go to church, my dad would throw rocks at me when I got home.'

"God showed me in that moment that my mother was an abused child, and I saw my mother differently from that moment on. It really changed my heart, and helped change my relationship with mom – it was a big awakening for me – and I think it helped Andrea change a little bit, as well."

A little bit, perhaps, but resentments still lingered – until two weeks ago, when Margaret Meeks, who died from breast cancer nine years ago at age 69, paid her oldest daughter a visit.

"Actually, it was my boyfriend that she came to see this time," Andrea says. "He has had nightmares all his life – spirits tormenting him – and what happened was, he told me one day, 'Your mom came to me.' And, of course, he never knew my mom. She was dead long before he and I were ever together.

"I said, 'Oh, yeah?' And he said, 'Yeah, she came and she told me that she was going to take away these nightmares, so that I can rest.' She said that she was always very jealous of me and my sister when she was alive, and now she wanted to help us – and help me – be happy.

"After having nightmares all his life, he has not had them since."

Both women say they have had untold numbers of similar experiences over the years, although Andrea has perhaps a little stronger connection to the spiritual world. She does not remember the first time a spirit appeared to her, but says it has been going on since she was a child.

"It runs in our family," she said.

"People I work with tease me all the time, and that's OK. But … my boss had two sisters who died. The first sister that died … there were no words. She's been my boss for a long time and we're close, and there just were no words.

"I make this art, and I have these cards. One of them has butterflies all over it, and I got that card and I wrote in there, 'Don't be sad. We'll all be together soon.' I gave her that card, and the next day at work, she said, 'You really are psychic, aren't you? My sister loved butterflies, and she told me before she died that we would all be together soon.'

Drew, mother of three and grandmother of four with another on the way, is working on a book about her father's Atlantic Ocean adventure in 1985 – he died two months after her mother, apparently of a broken heart – and she tells a story about a recent visit she is convinced he made to the family house in Gatesville, just north of Copperas Cove.

"I've been doing some writing, and I was trying to figure out when daddy came over to England (where she was stationed with the U.S. Air Force) the first time to buy the sailboat. He was a good letter writer, and so he wrote letters a lot, and I thought I would go and find these letters that he wrote to me back in 1985.

"Now, remember, it was 31 years ago, and 10 to 12 moves ago. I knew all the pictures and letters and stuff were probably in this one closet, where we had stacked boxes on top of boxes, on top of boxes. So I open the closet door, and on top of the first box is a shoe box in a (plastic) bag, full of letters from my dad.

"I take that box, and I look at the first letter on top of the pile, and it says, 'I wonder if the Sicilian has returned from her adventures …' I was in Sicily with the Air Force for a NATO exercise, so he was talking about me. Then, on the second page, it said, 'Big news. I bought a sailboat.'

"That was the letter I was looking for, and it was right there, on the very top of all those boxes. I know daddy put it there."

Another time, her mother paid a visit when no one was home, but left a calling card.

"My mother liked to remodel, and the bathroom was going to be her next project. After she died, my husband and I totally remodeled it. We went on a little trip to Houston, and when we came back, I put my stuff on the bed, and on my pillow is a triangular-shaped piece of the tile that we used in the bathroom.

"I asked my husband, 'Did you put this tile on the bed?' He said, no. I had made the bed before we left, and I know I didn't put a piece of tile on my pillow.

"I looked at him and said, 'Well, mom likes the bathroom.'"

Andrea, meanwhile, says her grandparents came to her in a dream the day before her mother died to try and prepare her for what was about to happen.

"They were real young, and they were holding hands. They came to me and they told me that mom was going to go with them. The next day, she died.

"I was asleep when they came to me, and when I got up and went downstairs, all the pictures fell off the wall. When a picture falls off the wall in your home, that's a foretelling that something is going to happen. Not necessarily death, but you need to be aware that something is going to happen. Birds coming to the window and trying to get in is another sign.

"Everybody has these things. It happens to everybody. Everybody has the same thing that I've got, it's just that you have to pay attention to it. I don't think I'm different from anybody else, really. I think I pay attention more," the mother of two and grandmother of two says.

"You don't have to believe it at all. It is what it is. That's the thing. I never try to convince anybody of anything, but if you start paying attention, you'll start to understand. If you start researching, you'll start to see that these things are happening to everybody.

"If you pay attention to the little things that happen in your life, the things that you call coincidences, you can figure it out. It's not really hard."

Conclusion

So there you go.

I hope you enjoyed reading this little collection as much as I enjoyed writing the stories and putting them all together for you. Like I said, pretty much everyone's got an interesting story to tell – they might just need someone like me to help them find it.

How about you?

Yes, that includes you. If you're interested, I can help you write your own story. Writing about people is my specialty. It's what I love to do, and I'd be happy to help you write your biography – the story of your life. Think about it. A nice little book that will be around forever and ever for your kids and grandkids, great-grandkids, great-great-grandkids to read.

Go to my website www.johnhenryiii.com and check out all my book titles, and you'll see what I do. There's also a section on my writing services. Just send me a little message and we'll talk. Let's do it!

And, by the way, if you don't mind, please take a minute and go write a book review on Amazon for this book. The more reviews a book gets, the more exposure it gets, and the more people get a chance to read it, and maybe find something that helps touch their life in some way. That's the real reward in all this for me. Connecting with people. After all, when you get right down to it, we're all pretty much the same inside, and want the same things – to feel loved, happy, and safe.

Thanks, again, and best wishes.

A Small Favor to Ask

Thanks for reading this collection; I hope you found these stories meaningful or helpful in some way. If you did, please take just a moment to write a brief review on Amazon. Your reviews mean a great deal to me, and they help others find this book, so that more readers can read these stories and perhaps find something in common with their own experience, and maybe even an answer of their own.

About the Author

John Henry Clark lives with his wife and a formerly stray and sweet but somewhat neurotic calico cat in a one-stoplight central Texas town, roughly halfway between Austin and Waco. A graduate of the University of Houston, Clark is an award-winning journalist, author, athlete, freelance writer, certified personal trainer, photographer, musician, and artist who has written more than a dozen non-fiction books, including his bestseller, *Camino: Laughter and Tears Along Spain's 500-mile Camino de Santiago*, which chronicles two of his three backpacking treks along the historic pilgrimage across northern Spain. A tireless seeker, researcher and questioner, John has written a number of other fascinating books dealing with the human experience, from tragedies to triumphs and more, including his first published title, *Finding God: An Exploration of Spirituality in America's Heartland,* and the riveting, *Depression Blues,* in which he talks about how he learned to overcome a lifelong struggle with depression and anxiety.

More from John H. Clark III

(For a complete listing of John's books, go to: https://www.johnhenryiii.com/my-books.html)

Buggy: The life and times of an 11-pound, four-legged, furry bundle of never-ending neuroses and undying love

Camino: Laughter and Tears along Spain's 500-mile Camino de Santiago

Darkness to Light: One woman's story of learning to live with crippling depression and finally finding happiness, inner peace and long-lasting love

Depression Blues: How to conquer sadness, loneliness, and despair -- you can live a happy life!

Destination Unknown: What Happens to Us When We Die? People from Around the World Weigh in On Humanity's Greatest Unsolved Mystery

Dying: A Father and Son Talk about Life, Regrets and Making up Lost Time

Everyday Heroes: Stories about ordinary Americans doing extraordinary things.

Finally Fit: It's never too late to achieve a dream

The Finally Fit Journal: a guided 90-day motivational journal and workbook designed to help you achieve your dreams

Finding God: An Exploration of Spiritual Diversity in America's Heartland

Gay Blues: Depression and anxiety from a life filled with prejudice, discrimination, rejection, and scorn can devastate homosexuals, but this often crippling trauma can be overcome

Peace of Mind: How to Be Happy and Positive in Troubled Times

People: Inside the lives of everyday folks from sea to shining sea

Simple Truth: You Are Enough – Learn to Love Yourself As You Deserve!

Sober in 30 Days: An experiment in alcohol-free living

The 30-Day Optimism Solution: How to Change from Pessimist to Optimist in 30 Days or Less

Today, I am thankful ...: a gratitude journal

Made in the USA
Columbia, SC
25 June 2021